Upward Bound

Upward Bound

Karl Gustafson

Filter Press, LLC

ISBN: 978-0-86541-271-2

Library of Congress Control Number: 2025905001

Cover design: Jordan Ellender
Cover image: The author on the Diamond of Longs Peak, 14,255 feet, in 1952
Photographs: All photographs courtesy of the Karl Gustafson Collection or Filter Press

Filter Press, LLC
Westcliffe, Colorado
https://www.filterpressbooks.com/

For my teenage climbing buddies

Preface

Coming of age for boys can bring chaos as their bodies ripen and their minds go independent. On the other hand, it can be a period of great exhilaration as they set off on bold new adventures. One can picture young Native American braves riding out on their first buffalo hunt.

I was lucky. Age thirteen found me moving from a small town in Iowa to Boulder, Colorado, and venturing forth with a band of young mountain climbers. We saved each other's lives and took on fierce rock faces and towering mountain peaks. Those contours and cliffs and our camaraderie shaped our hearts, minds, and souls.

This is that story.

From the introduction by William E. Siri, former president of the Sierra Club, in the book *Everest: The West Ridge,* by Thomas F. Hornbein (Sierra Club Ballantine Books 1968):

> Climbers tend to be rugged individualists. To them climbing is not a sport in the true sense, least of all an organized sport. Rather, it is a deep personal experience enjoyed to its fullest only when shared with a few close companions.

Prologue

Evening. High in the mountains. The tents are pitched. The Primus stoves are humming. Four teenage boys are gathered.

> Cory: "John, is the beef stew ready yet? We're all hungry!"
> Jim: "Hungrier! Hungrier!"
> John: "I'm working on it. I put two cans into the pot. They barely fit."
> Gus: "I hope it's enough. I could eat one can by myself!"

The next morning, early, before the climb to the summit:

> Cory: "Has anybody got more Spam ready to eat?"
> Gus: "Next time cook your own! Do you want some Grape-Nuts?"
> Cory: "Okay. Do you have any Carnation milk left for them?"
> Jim: "I've got another can if you want it."

Above them the morning sun had touched the high peaks. The strikingly pink alpenglow shone upon them invitingly.

Gus: "Let's get moving, guys."

1

I still remember the fine day seventy-five years ago, coming over American Legion Hill on the only main highway into the Boulder Valley and seeing the magnificent panorama open up in front of me. Although the foothills of the Front Range were still miles away to the west, the great snow peaks rising behind them took my breath away. I was only thirteen and had been reluctant to move here from Iowa, but immediately a rush of joy overtook me as I asked myself: *What is this place?*

But I said nothing as my father kept his foot on the gas pedal and we continued on the highway straight into Boulder. No one said anything. Our semi-affluent family had suddenly uprooted itself from a small, friendly farm town in Iowa to move here. No explanation had been given. My mother stoically sat in front of me and to my left my brother Dick, three years older. Dick had been taken out of an expensive military academy in Illinois and faced the prospect of entering his last year of high school here as a newcomer. I would be entering the eighth grade, my second year of junior high, also knowing nobody.

We continued straight into Boulder on Arapahoe Road and turned left onto 24th Street, the eastern boundary of Boulder. At the top of the 24th Street hill we turned left and headed east on a country dirt road. Quickly we came to our new home, the fourth house on the left. There was a new crushed-rock driveway into a small garage beside the house; it also looped back to the street in front of the house. There were only five houses on the left beyond 24th Street, as the road then descended past undeveloped land to a small intersection with another country dirt road, 28th Street.

It was June 1948, and Boulder was then a small college town nestled in a valley still dominated by its western mining roots, though its gold rush history was long past.

My father pulled the Buick off the little dirt road and onto the crushed red-rock loop in front of the house and wearily turned off the ignition key. We sat there. A little dust overtook us. No one said anything. It was hot outside. From the car we could see into the single picture window of the living room of the house. The house looked very small, a one-story, two-bedroom house into which the four of us would now move.

"Let's take a look," my brother growled as he hopped out of the car. He was always fast to action but did not look happy. That described him in general. My brother had an inner anger that influenced his outlook on everything.

We all got out. My father pulled a key out of his pocket and without saying anything opened the kitchen door to the house. As the others went in, I called out, "I'm going to look around outside awhile." I wasn't sure anyone heard me. It didn't matter.

I wandered into the backyard. Through it ran a small irrigation ditch, about eighteen inches wide. I bent down to dip my fingers into the current. Very fresh, cool mountain water coursed through. I looked more closely and saw tadpoles swimming to maintain their place against the current. That looked interesting. Behind the irrigation ditch was a row of small trees and then a flat, brown, scrappy-looking dry half acre. By the back fence was a small, abandoned pig shed about four feet high.

The air was very dry. I didn't mind, but I thought, *It could get really hot here!*

I walked back out front and gazed west toward the mountains. *I wonder what's up there?* I mused silently. It was very quiet, and the dust from our driving in had moved east with a slight breeze. There was no traffic. I looked across the street and saw a ranch house and small barn and fenced pasture running all the way down to 28th Street. There were two horses in the pasture, their tails swishing rhythmically at flies.

To our west there was a vacant lot and then an old house. I saw two old people sitting on the porch of the old house. I waved to them, and they waved back but did not get up. Dick came out and asked me, "Want to see our room?"

For the last two years, my brother had been attending the Western Military Academy in Alton, Illinois, as part of the grooming for a possible congressional appointment to West Point. That would be a big deal in our little town in Iowa. It had been said it might come down to my brother or Terry Schroyer, son of the businessman who ran the five-and-ten store in town. Terry had also been sent to Western for his proper prepping. My father had run the local hardware store in Manchester, a Gambles store. Congressional appointments to West Point from Iowa were said to go to the sons of local Republican businessmen.

"Sure," I replied. Then after a pause I asked, "Are you ready to go to high school here?"

"Don't know! Why?"

"I was just wondering. I suppose you're not going back to

Western this coming year?"

"Right. They have given up on the West Point idea."

I felt sorry for him as we headed into the house. The West Point thing had become an obsession for him. I felt sorry for myself having to share a bedroom with him for the next year. But I didn't say it.

We went through the side door of the house and into the small kitchen. There was a small dining table under the west window. The house had no separate dining room. Then there was the living room. Almost filling it was my mother's grand piano. She had insisted on shipping it out from Iowa, where we'd lived in a large two-story home. The new house was so small that we had not shipped much furniture. And it had no basement. Our new shared bedroom was barely large enough to hold our two single beds.

"I'll take the bed closest to the door," Dick said.

"Okay."

We looked around. There was nothing to see. We wandered back into the front two rooms of the house. My mother was busy unloading a box of pots and pans onto the small counter on the south wall of the kitchen and into small cabinets above.

"Bring your suitcases in boys, and I'll cook us some macaroni and cheese for dinner," she said.

My father was already in his small office next to the kitchen going through some papers spread out on his desk. He had arranged to be a life insurance salesman, taking over a retiring man's business, to be a new agent for the Equitable Life Insurance Company. He had never sold insurance before but was sure he could succeed. He once boasted to me that he could sell anything—not only items from a hardware store— by simply first spending twenty minutes convincing the customer to rely on his judgment. I believed him. My father was a terrific salesman.

I never felt close to my father. He was totally self-absorbed and distant. My brother and I could have been just his two employees.

My thoughts went back to our fine, much larger colonial-style house on Fayette Street in the small but prosperous town of Manchester. My father had made enough money from his Gambles store to move us from a smaller house on Butler Street to the new house on Fayette Street.

The Maquoketa River ran through Manchester. I yearned for the Maquoketa River to be there tomorrow so that I could hike down its forested banks and find a favorite sandbar to sit on and listen to the sound of its swift currents. Or to wander into its woods to look for a flying squirrel. Or to see how far downriver I could go and still get home before dark.

2

After dinner it was still light for a couple of hours, so I decided to walk down the road and south on 28th Street to explore my new surroundings. On the first hill the farmer's mailbox said "Babcock," and it looked like nobody was home. On the next hill the mailbox said "Reasoner." I wandered into the dirt driveway and saw a father and two boys working on some farm equipment near a tractor parked in front of a small barn.

"Hi," I called out as I waved to them. All three looked up and the older boy walked over.

"Hi. Who are you?"

"I'm Gus. My family and I just moved here from Iowa," I replied. "We bought the little white house over on Pennsylvania Avenue."

"What grade are you in?" the boy asked.

"Starting eighth grade in the fall," I replied.

"Me too! My name is Ross. Welcome to town."

There was a pause as we looked each other over. Then Ross asked, "Did you do Boy Scouts back in Iowa?"

"Yes. A lot."

"Do you want to go to our next Scout meeting? It's nearby on University Hill. I can take you over there."

"Sure!"

After another pause, Ross looked out across the pastures toward our house and inquired, "Do you know how to use your irrigation system?"

"That little ditch running through the backyard?"

"Yes. If you want, I'll come over tomorrow morning to show you how to use it."

"That would be great," I replied. "See you then."

It was getting darker, so I headed back home. As I walked along the dusty road, I noticed that the sun had set behind the mountains to the west, but the clouds above them still glowed with several shades of bright orange. There was some purple mixed in. I marveled at the sight, so different from the sunsets back home in Iowa. Colorado was a new world, and already I was excited to see what life here would bring.

* * *

My mother answered the door at eight o'clock the next morning. There stood my first new acquaintance in our new town.

"Hi! I'm Ross. Your son Gus came by our place last evening. Do you want to see how to work your irrigation system?"

"Why yes! Gus told me about you. Let me go get him," she answered, truly mystified by the prospect of a system for the little ditch of running water.

"Hey Ross, thanks for coming over."

"Sure thing, Gus. Let's go see if we can find your irrigation equipment. It's probably out in the garage."

Ross peered into our garage and located a wide canvas tube about 10 feet long and an accompanying board, and we made our way into the backyard. At the ditch, Ross stuck the board into the prepared slots in some concrete, and when the resulting dam started a buildup of water, he pushed the end of the canvas tube into the water and laid out its length into our backyard. Water flooded out into the yard. This was ditch irrigation!

"When you get the hang of it, you can probably even irrigate parts of your backyard where you have those fruit trees," Ross said triumphantly.

"Did you see how he did that?" my mother asked me.

"Yes. I can handle it!" I assured her.

* * *

The next week Ross and I walked across the nearly deserted University of Colorado (CU) campus to University Hill Junior High School, where Boy Scout Troop 72 met once a week. This was the same school where I would be attending eighth grade in the fall.

In Iowa there had been a great emphasis on Boy Scouts earning merit badges, and I was already a Star Scout. That first evening at my new Scout troop, I quickly picked up that the guys here couldn't care less about merit badges. Most were still at the lowest rank, Tenderfoot.

The troop scoutmaster was Mr. Swerdfeger, the father of the three Swerdfeger boys, Phil, Dave, and Gary. The second of the boys, Dave, welcomed me to the troop and said that he too would be entering eighth grade. Dave was pretty husky and told me he liked to play the end position on the football team.

"I'm pretty small," I ventured. "I've never played football."

"No problem," Dave replied. "There is a second, light-weight team. You look pretty fast. I'll bet you could play half-back on the lightweight team."

That sounded good to me. In a new town with new friends, I was happy to try new things.

Before the troop meeting began, we all played a game of pickup football in the yard in front of the school. University Hill Junior High sat right next to the busy street of Broadway, and the school's front yard was small and triangular. I thought it was an unusual place to play football, but no one else seemed to think so. Afterward we went into the little school gym for a short meeting. There was some talk about being a good citizen followed by a session on tying certain knots. Pretty soon, we were back outside playing more football in front of the school.

I thought, *This is a different kind of Scout meeting*. But I was glad to meet more boys my age and find a place for myself here. Most of these boys would become my classmates for years to come. Some would become my closest friends.

After the football practice ended, a few of us hung around. One boy approached me. "Hi. I'm John Clark," he announced. John was quite tall for his age and seemed sure of himself, like someone who knew his own mind. "Want to come over to my house tomorrow?"

"That sounds good. Where do you live?" I asked.

"Not far from here. At the corner of College and 10th Street," he said and gave me the address.

I was happy and somewhat relieved at how I was easily making new friends in Boulder. In Iowa, I'd left behind close friends I'd known all of my life, and I didn't think it would be so simple to start over with a new collection of friends. But already, the scene was looking promising.

The next day I went over to John's house at 10th Street and

College Avenue. It was a short walk from my house, just twenty minutes, cutting across the university campus and then through the small business district that served the Hill neighborhood. John's house was a modest one-story brick bungalow with a small apartment in the basement.

A pleasant-looking and somewhat plump lady greeted me at the door. "Hi Gus! Come on in. Welcome!" It was clear that John had told her I would be over. John's father and mother were never mentioned, but John referred to this woman, named Juanita, as Nita, and she cared for him like a mother, although it wasn't clear to me how they were related. Juanita was buoyant and cheerful and welcomed me as a new friend for John. He in fact became my first close friend in Boulder.

John came out of his room and said, "Hi, come on back." He did not look at me directly when he spoke and seemed introverted, even though friendly. I had also noticed that he had not played football with the same energy as the others at the Scout meeting the previous night.

John's room was neat, and there were some bookshelves and a desk in the corner. "I keep my own room the way I want it. Nita likes that," he volunteered. "Want to see my model planes?"

"Sure."

We turned to his desk where he had some uncompleted models of Piper Cubs and some others I could not quickly recognize. We fooled with them a bit. I had the feeling that John did not have many close friends. I also felt that we would get along just fine.

It seemed that John, being raised as an only child, had developed into a somewhat fastidious individual. But that did not bother me, as I tended to be a rather flexible team player, especially being a second-born with a sibling who wasn't easy-going.

Nita came in and asked if we both would like some ice cream. "Is it chocolate?" John asked.

"Yes, I have both chocolate and vanilla!" Nita said. She looked at me.

"I will take either one or both!" I assured her. We all laughed.

3

One day not long after I met John and Juanita in the summer of 1948, I pedaled my bicycle over to the Clark home looking for John. He was not there.

"John and George are up doing some climbing at the Second Flatiron," Juanita explained. "You can go find them up there."

The three main Flatirons comprise a row of jagged spires that tower more than 1,000 feet over the area of Chautauqua Park, on the west side of Boulder. I already knew where the Second Flatiron was by sight, but I had not gone there until now. Climbing steep sheer rock faces wasn't something I had even dreamed about doing back in Iowa. Now it sounded like something both intriguing and natural. Why not climb up the rocky faces of cliffs?

George Hall, a nearby neighbor of John's, had bought a 120-foot heavy hemp rope, which climbers still used in those days. He was two years older than John and I. He had been talking to the rock climbers at the university, according to Juanita, and he already had some climbing experience. But this was John's first exposure to rock climbing, as it would be for me.

Without hesitation I rode my bicycle up 10th Street to Baseline Road and then up the steep, narrow road to the Bluebell Shelter, below the Second Flatiron. I could see the Second Flatiron towering above me. I followed a short trail to the base of the rock and looked up.

I saw John and George up on the steep face. They were sitting about one-third of the way up, fiddling with the rope.

"Can I join you?" I shouted up.

"Come on up," George shouted down, as he spotted me. "Do you need the rope?"

"I don't think so," I replied. I easily climbed up to them in my street shoes.

"Wow! You don't even have boots or your tennis shoes on!" George exclaimed.

"Well, I wasn't planning on this," I replied with a laugh. But the climb had not been hard for me, and I was game.

The Flatiron cliffs were formed from a former seabed that tilted up at an average angle of 55 degrees, and although eroded to some extent, they do not usually have good hand- or footholds. One clings to them by the friction of one's boot soles and hands. The Second Flatiron is easier than the others and more broken up than the First and Third Flatirons. But still, if you happened to come off, you would fall several hundred feet to your death.

We casually learned to belay each other with the stiff hemp rope as we eventually made our way toward the top. We climbed up between the two large overhanging summit blocks. Then, because we wanted to summit, we climbed a short steep pitch up the right face of the highest point of the Flatiron. We had no climbing harnesses but simply tied in with an overhand knot to the rope around our waist.

"Congratulations, you two!" George said, complimenting

us on our first climb.

The view from the top was extraordinary. You could see all of Boulder and the vast plains extending forever out east. There were quite a few little lakes.

"I think I can see American Legion Hill. That was how we drove into Boulder," I pointed out.

"Right. Just out east on Arapahoe," John chipped in.

"Amazing how the mountains just rear up out of the plains," George observed. John and I nodded in agreement. The landscape here was simply extraordinary.

After about half an hour of appreciating our vantage point, George showed John and I how to wrap the rope around our body and do a short rappel to the ground behind the Second Flatiron. We did not have any pitons or carabiners, but George found a rock knob we could use to anchor our simple Dulfer-style rappel down. Then we picked our way down the boulder slope between the First and Second Flatirons to arrive back at the Bluebell Shelter.

It was my first rock climb. It seemed quite natural to me. And I was hooked. I could not wait for our next climb.

* * *

For the rest of that first summer in Boulder, George, John, and I continued our rock climbing self-instruction at the Gregory Canyon Amphitheatre spires of the Flatirons. We taught ourselves how to belay, how to find routes up a rock cliff, and how to rappel down them. We climbed in our basketball shoes and still used the thick hemp rope. There were not many other rock climbers in that era, and often we could go up by ourselves, no one else in sight, and just try anything.

One day when John and I were climbing a cliff in the Amphitheatre, I heard a *whoosh* go by my head. I looked down and did not see any rock crashing into the ground.

"Strange! Something just went past my head! Not a rock!" I shouted out.

"Duck hawk!" John answered. "They nest in the Flatirons. They can go two hundred miles per hour! Fastest things alive!"

* * *

As we gained experience, John and I became more ambitious in our climbs and more confident of our abilities. There was so much terrain to explore, and we were always thinking of new challenges. One that we wondered about was the top of the First Pinnacle of the Amphitheatre, going up its south ridge. There is a little cave in the bottom of the Amphitheatre, and you could start climbing a steep but easy chimney above it until you were just below the top of the pinnacle on its south side. Above that was a very narrow, vertical ridge pitch of no more than twenty feet high and about a yard wide to the top.

One day we decided to try it.

"It looks pretty vertical. And I don't see any holds," John observed.

I was undeterred by this for some reason. "I want to lead it!" I declared forcefully. I had not led a difficult pitch before, but that day I somehow felt very confident of my abilities. Most likely there was some adolescent ego involved.

"Okay," John replied as he uncoiled the rope. "I will belay you. Let's both tie in with bowline knots."

Very exposed and with an unsecured belay that could not hold me if I fell—and would pull John off as well—I moved up the thin spire largely by will, balancing on some tiny foot- and handholds to my left and right on the edge of the thin vertical face.

Halfway up I was stopped by seeing nothing above me to hold onto. There was no way I could climb back down, and I knew that. The situation started to feel rather desperate as I concentrated on maintaining my delicate balance, spread eagle on the thin rib.

"I don't see anything. No holds," I shouted down to John, my recent overconfidence quickly vanishing.

"Look harder," John replied firmly.

I looked harder as I delicately balanced on whatever was holding me to the rock. Then I saw a couple of small fingerholds, and with a huge sigh of relief I pulled myself up and over onto the top. This was a tiny, perhaps previously unclimbed pitch that had tested me to the limit. As with my other climbs, it made me hungry for more.

4

"Do you want to go on a backpack trip with John and an expert?" Nita asked me one day in early September when I arrived at the Clark home. As usual, I was game for a new adventure in the magnificent Rocky Mountains. I said yes with enthusiasm.

School did not start until later in September. The peach harvest on the Western Slope depended on youth labor from Boulder and other eastern Colorado cities to bring in the peaches just as they ripened to perfection in late August and September. So our school year began after the crops were brought in.

The basement apartment of Juanita's small house was rented to a University of Colorado student named Walt Sticker. Walt was an experienced climber. In early September of 1948, a nice stretch of late summer had Juanita convincing Walt to take John and me on a four-day backpacking trip over the Continental Divide before school started.

I'm not sure if it was out of kindness, if Walt really enjoyed our company, or if Juanita offered him a rent discount for the favor. But Walt immediately got into the spirit and gathered

John and me in his basement room and advised us on what supplies we would need.

I had saved a little money from mowing a few lawns around town and selling fresh watercress, which I collected from the irrigation ditches and sold to Tripp's market on the Hill. With my small savings, I went to the Boulder Army Store downtown and bought a mummy sleeping bag, rucksack, and rain poncho. All were used but in reasonable condition. And very easy on the billfold.

Carefully I packed up my gear the night before our trip, checking to make sure I had everything on my penciled list. It was not much: an extra shirt and gloves thrown in, some socks. We all had canteen belts to wear, since at higher altitudes in the more remote mountains, you could safely drink the water from any rivulet you could find.

Early the next morning, well before daylight, Juanita drove the three of us up to Brainard Lake, at an elevation of 10,400 feet, and deposited us at the end of the road, wishing us well.

To the west was total wilderness. "Let's go!" Walt shouted enthusiastically as he slung his rucksack over his shoulders. I did the same and noticed that my pack fit well. It had a light metal frame and some writing scrawled on the side by its previous owner, a soldier in World War II. Already, everything felt right and like this was exactly where I belonged.

We were at the beginning of the Pawnee Pass Trail. Dawn had broken, and the trail was not steep. A beautiful lake, Long Lake, was to our left. The weather looked favorable. The air had a freshness that contained the strong scent of pine trees.

Walt set a fast pace for about a mile and then stopped and turned around to see how John and I were doing. "There is a short climb now up to Isabelle Lake," he said. "Are you guys doing okay?"

"Doing okay," John replied.

"No problem," I added.

Several switchbacks brought us to Isabelle Lake, which was at timberline. Walt did not stop and led us up a hill on the right side, bringing us to a steep buttress. "It gets steep now," Walt yelled out. "Lots of switchbacks!"

"No problem!" I shouted back.

With our heads down to see the placement of our feet on the narrow trail, which dropped off steeply below us with plenty of exposure, we reached the top of the buttress.

"Let's have a little water," Walt finally directed. "How are you guys doing?"

"No problem," John replied quickly.

"How about you, Gus?"

"No problem."

After a short water break without bothering to sit down, the three of us continued on a gradually rising trail to the west. A breeze blew straight into our faces, but no storm clouds could be seen ahead of us. Without stopping, Walt in a loud voice proclaimed, "That's Pawnee Peak to our right. That's Isabelle Glacier and Navajo Peak to our left."

Pawnee Peak did not appear very high as I snuck a peek at it. But Navajo Peak looked quite forbidding with its turret-like conical top reaching high above.

"I can't see Isabelle Glacier!" John shouted.

"You can see the top of it. If you want to see the whole thing we would have to go over to the edge here and look down," Walt replied.

"That's okay, let's keep going for now," John said.

Eventually we arrived at a small sign that said, "Pawnee Pass, 12,542 feet." Ahead of us the trail could be seen dropping steeply down in a series of switchbacks.

"Is this the Continental Divide?" I asked.

"Yep. Water here flows down west to the Pacific Ocean."

Walt then quickly slung his pack back on, and we started down the steep trail. There was not a lot of talking, just the sound of our footsteps and breathing as we moved in unison along the trail. After many switchbacks we could see across a valley a grand cirque of peaks, with Fair Glacier and the striking 11,900-foot high Lone Eagle Peak in the center.

It was a beautiful view that nobody would see unless they had come up over the Divide and dropped down into the western slope as we had. Lone Eagle Peak was named after Charles Lindbergh and was sometimes called Lindbergh Peak. It had a spearpoint shape with a dramatic north face. To its left and a bit farther back was the near-vertical Fair Glacier. Apache Peak, as high as Navajo, closed the cirque on its east end.

I was thunderstruck and stood there transfixed in my stance. So did John. Even Walt was taken in by the panorama that unfolded before us.

My thoughts went back to Iowa. There were some nice little hills there. But I could see I was in a new world here.

A light breeze cooled us. Our pack straps bit into our shoulders, but we did not mind.

"Just below Lone Eagle Peak there's a small lake named Crater Lake," Walt added. "We might camp a bit below that."

Walt found the small side trail that branches south into the cirque and led us up less than a mile to a little meadow below the peak and glacier.

"We'll camp here!" Walt exclaimed, almost joyously.

We had no tents. There was ample room to lay out our ponchos with sleeping bags on top of them. Immediately we were overtaken by swarms of mosquitoes. After cold sandwiches for dinner, we curled into our sleeping bags. As dark descended we could hear the porcupines in the trees and bushes near us. "Don't worry about the porcupines. They won't bite!" Walt offered gratuitously from under his poncho.

"I am not worried about them biting me! What about their quills?" John shot back.

"Just don't reach out to them!" Walt said.

Soon we were all asleep, not worried about porcupines or anything.

The next morning Walt set his sights on Apache Peak, which summits at 13,441 feet. We had no climbing gear. No ice axes and no rope. But Walt's idea was for us to somehow make our way up the left edge of the steep Fair Glacier. If we could get up that, we could then see if we could continue farther up Apache's southwest ridge, to the top of the peak. Walt had not been in this valley before, and what he proposed was not a known route.

"I haven't done this before. I hope it will go!" Walt admitted.

"Let's get started," I said.

"Okay! That's the attitude! You guys follow me and don't get far behind!" Walt commanded.

It was not very far hiking up the meadows until we came up against the cliff holding Fair Glacier. It was a hanging glacier, and it would be suicidal to go out onto it with no ice axes.

"Just watch your step, climb slowly but stay close to me, and use your hands anytime!" Walt warned.

Without any equipment, the climbing was primitive and even savage at times as we individually propped ourselves between the steep cliff wall on the left and the glacier's edge on the right.

"You guys all right?" Walt called out after a few feet.

"No problem," both John and I replied.

We slowly clawed our way up to the top of the left side of Fair Glacier. A nice small portion of flat ridge-top greeted us.

It had taken a lot of concentration to climb that glacier-cliff route, but the exposure as we climbed had not bothered me.

"Let's take a water break here," said Walt as he sat down on a small boulder.

John and I found small boulders to sit on. A nice breeze wafted by us. There were no human voices to disturb us. The pure serenity of this wild place was remarkable. How wonderful to be away from it all!

"That's Wheeler Basin on the other side. Sometimes it is called Hell Hole!" Walt joked, looking south. "No trails. But if you look closer you can see just beyond it a trail heading up Arapaho Pass. We'll be camping over there tomorrow night."

John and I looked south and John turned to me.

"Want to hike up into Hell Hole sometime, Gus?"

"I don't know, John. We can get a better look tomorrow night when we're over there," I replied.

John broke out laughing, exclaiming, "No way I am going up into a place called Hell Hole!"

I appreciated John's rare sense of humor. But as I looked over at the vast expanse of Hell Hole, I felt a sense of adventure at the prospect of going there sometime. A kind of explorer's joy crept into my senses.

Walt turned his attention to the west ridge of Apache Peak, which rose to the east of us. It was not intimidating and did not look very long. "Looks a little loose but not bad," he said and started up. The ridge was easy compared to what we had just come up. Soon we were atop Apache Peak.

It felt good to be on Apache, even though by then it was late in the afternoon. To our south, Navajo's sharp conical summit on the Divide was about the same height, at 13,409 feet. In between was the top of Navajo Glacier, which fell off steeply to the east.

I felt a bit overwhelmed. This was my first mountain

climb, and it had been thrilling.

"Have you climbed Navajo?" John asked Walt.

"Nope. And I've never been here before either," Walt replied somewhat wistfully.

"You've never been up the usual route up Apache on its east side?" I inquired.

"Nope. That's why we came into this country, to see it, climb a peak," Walt said.

The view was breathtaking. Looking to the north, we could see the top of Isabelle Glacier and beyond that Mount Audubon, which at 13,229 feet sat a bit lower than Apache. Far to the north was Longs Peak, at 14,259 feet, an iconic Colorado 14er. The North Face of Longs Peak's neighbor Mount Meeker, at 13,916 feet, combines with Longs Peak's East Face to form a magnificent cirque that is one of the key attractions of Rocky Mountain National Park.

After quick snacks of peanut butter sandwiches that Nita had made for us and more water, we started down the rocky west ridge of Apache that we had climbed up.

"Be careful. This route has not been gardened. The rocks are loose. It's trickier going down," Walt advised.

When we got to the little saddle at the top of Fair Glacier, we looked down at the almost vertical glacier and the cliffs holding it to the ridge. It looked more forbidding than it had looked coming up.

Walt announced, "Here we go down the same way we came up! Don't go out onto the glacier. It is too steep and icy." We inched our way down, again with Walt in the lead to pick the best handholds on the cliffs to our right. With great relief we paused at the bottom.

"That was something!" John blurted out to Walt.

"Pretty steep, all right!" Walt agreed.

Dusk overtook us as we strode out from the base of the

glacier. But we were able to find our camp.

It was another night sleeping in the open with the porcupines and mosquitoes, but we slept well, and then we were up early for a long backpack down Cascade Creek and then up the next valley to camp in a lush meadow below Mount Achonee (12,649 feet), with Arapaho Pass (11,906 feet) to our left. We had been lucky and had had no rain on the trip due to the clear Second Summer weather of that September.

"Can you see Hell Hole up to our north now?" Walt asked, as John and I strained our eyes but could see no hint of any trails.

"It might be fun to explore up there sometime," John said, partially rebuking his protestation the day before. "But let's organize camp here now." John as usual was more interested in practical matters than in fantasy.

After a comfortable night with no porcupines and only a few mosquitoes, the next day we went over Arapaho Pass to meet Nita and her car at the agreed-upon pickup point, the Fourth of July Campground at 10,100 feet, at the top of a rough dirt road.

Nita was clearly glad to see us. She offered us cups of hot chocolate and asked how the trip had gone.

"They did well," Walt assured her.

"Well, they both look well," Nita replied as she looked at John and me. I nodded affirmatively.

John nodded too. "Thanks, Nita, for the peanut butter sandwiches, which we ate both days."

"Even for breakfast and dinner too!" I agreed.

Walt added, looking at Nita, "I cooked macaroni and cheese for one dinner, but we wanted to keep it simple, Nita!"

After the drive back to Boulder, Nita dropped me off at our house. Neither my dad nor Dick was home. My mother was happy to see me safe and sound. I was supremely happy.

5

The first day at University Hill Junior High School finally arrived in late September, and I was excited. Boulder was a much bigger place than the little town of Manchester in Iowa. Manchester had numbered only about four thousand inhabitants, mostly merchants serving the farm community and a lot of retired farmers.

At the Valentine Hardware store in downtown Boulder, at the corner of Broadway and Pearl Street, the entire east wall of the store advertised in a large painted mural: "Boulder. 19,999 inhabitants, including 8,000 university students."

Although Boulder was a small city, it was decidedly a city rather than a town like Manchester. At the Scout meetings, I had noticed that the junior high building was about twice the size of Manchester's High School building. And Boulder had two junior highs, whereas Manchester had only one.

Ross Reasoner came by our little house early that morning, and we set out together. We cut across the university campus heading west, just as we did for Scout meetings. Back then, 24th Street formed the eastern border of the university campus, and a short distance south of our house, the university had just built the new Aden, Brackett, and Cockerel dormitory buildings on the west side of the street. We cut west of them and to the east of Baker Hall and quickly found ourselves directly across Broadway from our school, which everyone called Uni Hill. We did not even think about the college students as we wove our way through them and their campus.

Dave Swerdfeger and some of the other Boy Scouts I'd gotten to know welcomed me to their school. It felt good seeing the familiar faces, and I already knew the school a little from Scout meetings. The principal was Ted Hovde, a rather small but dignified man. When I arrived at my first class, social studies, immediately Mrs. Blake welcomed me and introduced me to the whole class. She was clearly a school community leader.

All the Uni Hill classes seemed easy to me. The schools in Iowa had been noticeably more advanced. Here I could sit back and enjoy the new setting and new kids. Besides social studies and my other classes, such as geography, also taught by Mrs. Blake, there was a shop class in the basement of the building. Our shop teacher was Mr. Butler, who was quite friendly to all of the students.

In general, the Uni Hill students did not seem much preoccupied with their academics. Boulder had too much else to offer. For one thing, the mountains rose up quickly a few blocks to the west. That was already my own preoccupation, but I also wanted to find where I would fit in at school, both socially and as a student.

Across Broadway from my new school were a few houses that had been converted into informal lunch cafés for the junior high students, since Uni Hill had no cafeteria of its own. You could brownbag it, but we teenagers preferred to congregate across the street, where we could get hot dogs and drinks rather cheaply.

After school on that first day was the first football practice. I was as excited and nervous about the tryouts as I was about school. But as Dave Swerdfeger had predicted, I easily qualified for the lightweight team. Full pads, helmets, and shoes were issued immediately to all of us on the lightweight and heavyweight teams.

Meanwhile, a rather muscular member of the heavyweight team made his way over to me. "Hi. I'm Jim Vickery. I'm the quarterback on the heavyweight team," the sturdy boy announced.

"Pleased to meet you!" I replied enthusiastically.

Jim went on, "Hey, I've heard you are a mountain climber?"

"I'm learning. I've only been doing it this summer," I answered, not feeling that I was any kind of expert.

"Some of my friends and I would like to learn how to climb. Would you be willing to show us what you know?"

"Sure," I replied. "How about this Saturday?"

"Great! I'll see if I can get my brother John and my friend Cliff over too," Jim replied before heading back over to the heavyweight team. Then Mr. Hovde separated the two teams to practice on the small lawn in front of the school, as we did at Boy Scout meetings.

The lightweight team's quarterback was Dick Swann. That first day he took me under his wing and said, "Gus, you look pretty fast. You can be left halfback."

I had never played football before coming to Boulder, but the plays were few and easy to learn.

In Manchester, basketball had been the main sport. I can still remember the radio announcer of the University of Iowa games exclaiming, "Murray Wier is driving to the basket!" The new coach in Manchester had organized early morning seventh-grade special practices for a few of us before school began. Basketball was king in Iowa in those days. I was pretty good, learning the new one-handed jump push shot with no trouble. I would have been first team for sure in the high school there.

There were no basketball games in the little Uni Hill gym, although some of the guys got permission to play some pickup basketball after school. Later on I would join them a few times, but I was too small to be much of a rebounder, even though my shooting was pretty good.

Uni Hill also possessed no track, although a few meets were held on the school's front yard. I was pretty fast, but others were faster.

* * *

Saturday morning came quickly and I went over to the Vickery house at 1035 Eighth Street, just below Flagstaff Mountain. The Vickerys' small home was not far from John Clark's, just a few blocks to the west. In between on College Avenue was George Hall's house. His mother had remarried someone named Segur from Chicago. George was not in the Scout troop; nor were the Vickerys.

"Hello! Come in!" Jim's mother welcomed me. The house looked tiny, but Jim's mother's charm overwhelmed me. She was quite small compared to Jim but effused great warmth. Jim scrambled up the small stairs from his bedroom in the basement and shouted, "Hi Gus!"

Jim told me that his mother was closely related to the Groucho Marx family. In a sense, she looked it. She would quickly become a mother figure to all of us. We fondly called her Mamoo. Jim then volunteered that his father, Howard, was a stonemason who had been born into a mining family high in the mountains in the little town of Alma, at 10,578 feet the highest town in the United States. Alma was over by Fairplay in the 10,000-foot high South Park plateau in central Colorado.

Howard was having coffee in the small kitchen behind the living room.

"Hi Gus, welcome to our house!" he boomed. He was a large man and strongly built.

Howard had been a hard-rock miner in the high mines of the Mosquito Mountain Range, west of Alma. Some of those mines went all the way up to the tops of the peaks, at 14,000 feet. When the mines played out, Howard had moved his family to Boulder and learned the art of stonemasonry.

Howard was half Cherokee. The other half was from Cornwall, England, where many of the mining families in Colorado had come from.

Just then Jim's non-identical twin brother, John, came in the front door.

"Hi guys. Are we going to talk a little mountain climbing?"

"You bet! Nice to meet you," I responded.

Jim showed his Native American genes very clearly. John did not at all, although his skin was a little darker than most of us.

Jim and John shared a tiny bedroom that had been carved out of the foundation of the house. We went down there. A few minutes later there was a knock on the door upstairs. Mamoo answered it and hollered down to us, "It's Cliff! Shall I send him down?"

"Cliff, old buddy! Get on down here!" Jim commanded.

Cliff Chittim lived on the Hill at 11th and Aurora with his Aunt Latorra, who had volunteered to raise him after his mother died. They lived about four blocks from the Vickerys.

Cliff crowded into the little room and greeted me with a genuine wide smile. I had met him already through Scouts. Cliff was of medium build and immediately likeable.

"Will Bill be coming over?" Cliff asked.

"I doubt it," John answered promptly. "I think his mother would prefer that he not get too heavy into climbing."

Bill Fairchild was an only child and lived in a fancy house that his mother, a lawyer, had built just above Baseline Road at 10th Street. Bill's father was a musician who had played in the Glenn Miller Orchestra. Bill himself was already a talented musician and played drums in musical quartets. Later Bill would join our group.

That first day in the small bedroom of the Vickery twins, I looked around at my new friends and immediately liked all of them. They seemed serious about doing some climbing and learning all they could. It was clear that Mamoo would not stand in the way.

* * *

Back at school, football practices continued on the small front lawn of Uni Hill for the next few weeks, and then we would face Casey Junior High for the first time that season. The game would be played on Boulder High School's full-size official football field. Boulder High was the only high school in Boulder, and Casey and Uni Hill were the only junior high schools.

Casey Junior High was across town and about the same size as Uni Hill. I had not met anyone yet from Casey. Boulder was effectively split apart by Boulder Creek and the down-town shopping district. I and all of my friends at that time lived in what was South Boulder.

The football game turned out to be rough even though we

were "lightweights." The preparation emphasis by both coaches had been on blocking and tackling, learning the fundamentals so that you could qualify for the Boulder High School team in later years. Football was serious business in Boulder, as basketball had been in Manchester.

No scores occurred in the first half of the game.

Then, in the third quarter, Uni Hill approached the Casey goal line. Dick Swann took me aside and said quietly, "Gus, I will fake right and then shovel the ball over to you. You go like hell. The guys will block for you."

"Okay. Let's go!" I agreed.

After taking the ball from center, Dick faked a handoff to his right, saw both teams flow over in that direction, spun around, and saw me. As I moved left, he expertly shovel-passed the ball to me. Terrified, with glazed eyes, I saw a lot of Casey bodies on the ground between me and the goal line. As fast as I could, I sped between them to score a touchdown. The team all gathered around to congratulate me. The moment was golden. I felt like a hero, and Uni Hill went on to win the game.

* * *

As fall progressed, Uni Hill scheduled the first dance for the eighth grade. It was held immediately after school, and we were all required to come down to the small gym. The boys all gravitated to one side and lined up against the wall. The girls were all on the other side. The gym was quite small, and there was not much distance between the two sides.

Mr. Hovde was there. Mrs. Blake was there. Music was playing. But nothing was happening. Smiling widely, Mrs. Blake looked at the girls' side of the room and directed, "Why don't some of you girls go over and pick a boy and we can all learn to dance!"

A good-looking girl named Jan Davis stepped forward and came over and picked out Dave Swerdfeger. A few other girls followed and made their selections. Nobody picked me.

Mrs. Blake in her dominant voice called out, "All of you now! Find a partner! I will show you the two-step dance."

Some girl came over and grabbed me, and out onto the floor we went. The school's first eighth-grade dance did not last long. We had to do a couple more dances. Then with great relief we were outside practicing as football teams again.

6

There was a national election in the fall of 1948 and on November 3, 1948, the *Chicago Daily Tribune* published the huge front-page headline:

DEWEY DEFEATS TRUMAN

The headline of course was incorrect. Truman, a Democrat, defeated Dewey to become the 33rd U.S. President. As he began his presidential term, Truman would sometimes hold that *Chicago Daily Tribune* front page in front of him with a wide smile.

Governor Thomas E. Dewey of New York had been heavily favored to win the election, even though he had lost to Franklin D. Roosevelt in 1944. Anyone would have lost to FDR at that time, during World War II.

Truman had been FDR's vice president and took over just as World War II was concluding. With no apologies, Truman had okayed the atomic bombs dropped on Hiroshima and Nagasaki in 1945, to convince the Japanese emperor, Hirohito, to lean on his military diehards and agree to surrender. All but five of Japan's larger cities had been reduced to ashes by General Curtis LeMay's firebombing campaign. The hardcore Japanese military did not know how to stop a war. So Hirohito just stepped up and saved what little of Japan was left.

Dewey had been a famous and extremely effective racketbuster as district attorney in New York before he became governor. He was a very smooth talker and the upper-class candidate. Polished and well-dressed and with an elegant small mustache, he had been considered a shoo-in.

Harry Truman was not FDR and spoke his opinions openly.

In Iowa, everyone I had known was a Republican, including my parents. When it turned out that Truman had won the election in 1948, they were aghast.

"How can that be?" my father fumed. "Dewey would be a much better president!"

My mother nodded, and they both just sat there at the kitchen table looking thunderstruck.

I kept my mouth shut but felt some of my first political feelings. My feelings were pro-Truman. I had never liked the newsreels and press favoring of Dewey, who seemed to me to be too smooth.

Truman, on the other hand, had a feisty streak. He had pulled off the upset by carrying out a barnstorming train campaign. He would stand at the back of the train and speak to all the small-town folk that the rails took him to through the center of America. It was an effective strategy. I was not the only one who felt that Dewey was "too smooth."

Probably I was the first Democrat in the Gustafson or Anderson (my mother's side) lineages. I never mentioned any politics at home. My father would have gone off the rails with his quick temper.

The period of 1948 to 1953 was the height of the Cold War,

between the West, led by the United States, and the East, led by the Soviet Union. The Soviets blocked the western allies' railway, road, and canal access to their sectors of Berlin in June of 1948 to protest the new West German Deutschmark that the allies had brought into Berlin. Truman responded with a massive airlift of food and goods for the people of Berlin. American and British cargo planes flew over Berlin or into Tempelhof Airfield more than 250,000 times in the next year to sustain the German people in their sectors of Berlin. This broke the Soviet blockade.

It was not widely known that Truman had been an artillery officer in World War I and had seen plenty of action. He did not emphasize it in his campaign. Later he said that his whole political career was based on his war service and war associates.

* * *

Dick had made a splash into Boulder High School's 1948–1949 senior class by being something of a daredevil. One day we went up to see him ski at the small rope tow that served a ski slope at Chautauqua Park. We could pick him out as he came charging straight down the hill. Dick had never skied before.

As he approached Baseline Road, he just kept going and crashed into some cars parked beside the road. He picked himself up, grinned at us, and headed up the rope tow again.

There was enough snow falling on Boulder in those days to sustain that small ski area on the lower Enchanted Mesa area just above Baseline Avenue.

* * *

The Boy Scout troop I had joined would soon bring more mountain adventures into my life. Mr. Swerdfeger, the scoutmaster, was a full-time state highway patrolman, and on weekends he worked at his small mine up in Boulder Canyon.

When Mr. Swerdfeger was driving us Scouts somewhere along the high gravel Peak to Peak Highway, west of Boulder at 8,000 feet, he would sometimes purposely almost slide off the road at high speed on a corner. Barely saving us from going off a cliff, he would turn his head to look back at us and ask, "Did you boys like that!?"

"Pretty close!" someone would respond.

He wanted to impress us with his driving prowess and did. But he enjoyed the close calls too. Mrs. Swerdfeger was a good-looking woman who had given birth to three sons separated in age by two years each. She had her hands full raising that family in a little white stucco house on 15th Street, about two blocks above the Uni Hill school.

A California company had started marketing a three-wheeled automobile called the Davis Divan. It was a promotional fraudulent scheme, and only thirteen Divans were ever built. Mr. Swerdfeger somehow managed to arrange to drive one in a parade in Boulder in 1948. We all were looking forward to seeing our scoutmaster wheeling a Davis along the streets of Boulder.

The Davis was a funny-looking little futuristic green convertible and could turn on a dime. I don't know if it was stable at high speed. We were thrilled to see Mr. Swerdfeger swirling it around as the parade came up Broadway to pass Uni Hill.

During Christmas vacation that year, Mr. Swerdfeger took some of the Scout troop up to spend a few days at the Swerdfeger family cabin in the historic mining town of Ward. At an elevation of 9,450 feet, Ward was twenty-two miles west of Boulder. The Swerdfeger family had a little cabin situated on the hill on the south side of Ward.

The eight of us Scouts were to be left there for a week under the supervision of a college student from CU who Mr. Swerdfeger had unofficially commissioned as an assistant scoutmaster. Ross Reasoner and John Clark were among the guys in this group.

The snow in Ward was very deep that winter of 1948–1949. Each day we would trudge over to the Olson store in the old train depot in the north side of Ward to get supplies. Mrs. Olson always had something for us to take back to our cabin, at least milk and bread. Mrs. Olson was famous for her freshly baked pies. The Peak to Peak Highway passed directly in front of the old depot store, and motorists in summer would always stop to have a piece of one of Mrs. Olson's pies.

At that time, there were only seventeen permanent residents in Ward, a town that once boasted seven thousand inhabitants. One of those few inhabitants was Cody, a thirteen-year-old and the only boy in town. He was overjoyed to see us. He showed us the Ward sledding hill, which was short and quite steep. You had to use your feet and hands to stop yourself. Ward, like many of the old mining towns, just hangs there in the end of a high mountain valley.

We kept warm by feeding pieces of the many logs we cut into the single stove that had to heat the whole Swerdfeger dwelling. I got pretty good at swinging an ax down into the log to split the wood into kindling and pieces of manageable size. There was no scouting purpose of the trip. The only apparent goal was to survive.

The CU student who had been drafted into being an assistant scoutmaster had no expertise, but he did his best to lecture us a few times about knots and felt his main task was to keep us alive and uninjured.

* * *

Returning to Boulder, I found that the Gustafson family had made no plans at all for Christmas. My mother played Christmas tunes on her grand piano in the small living room. Dick and I tried to stay warm by standing with our backs very close to the rudimentary wall gas heaters that were supposed to heat the whole house. My father was seldom at home, as he was out talking anyone he could find into buying Equitable Life Insurance.

"Any Christmas decorations this year? No tree?" I asked my mother.

"We haven't gotten around to that yet," she replied. "Maybe next year." She did not elaborate that my dad, my brother, and even me were just not around to provide any Christmas spirit, so she wasn't going to bother.

* * *

Some boys in our eighth-grade class had ties to the mountain town of Nederland, and among them was John Clark. At one time there was a four-story Clark Mill at the little town of Tungsten, just below Nederland. The Clark family had land and mining claims on the high hill just north of the mill, which was aptly named Hurricane Hill. Nita would sometimes take John and I up there to spend a few nights in a converted mine shed next to a little pond called Dry Lake. We would explore the mines and cabins nearby. Most of the cabins had not yet collapsed and contained beautiful iron four-burner wood stoves.

But no matter how high, cold, and windy, Ward became my favorite mountain town, and it would remain so my whole life. At 9,450 feet, it is the highest still-inhabited old mining town in Boulder County. During the rebellious Vietnam War years, it became a haven for antiwar hippies. Throughout its history, conscientious townsfolk have maintained the Columbia Hotel, which still stands today. The hotel is named for the fabulous Columbia silver vein.

* * *

In spring of 1949, as the mountain snows melted and the creeks approached flood stage, some of the Boulder High daredevils decided to go up Boulder Canyon some distance and try to float down in little rubber life rafts. My brother and a companion made their way down and were soon in big trouble. While his friend managed to grab a tree limb and pull himself out, Dick was alone in the raft as it came barreling down the rushing Boulder Creek a few miles west of Boulder.

Some fellow Boulder High students watching from cars on the Boulder Canyon highway quickly raced down to Boulder and alerted the police and fire departments that Dick was on his way down, out of control and in trouble. An emergency squad gathered at the 24th Street Bridge, which had no clearance between it and the water. There they managed to pull Dick from the raft as it hit the bridge. Dick treated the whole incident with his usual nonchalance.

Dick had made friends with Chuck Gathers, the star halfback on the Boulder High football team. Chuck's father ran the local Nash Rambler automobile shop. Some models of the Rambler had a convertible bed as the backseat. We all thought that might be great for camping before a climb. But the Ramblers had a very low clearance underneath, which would not work well on rough mountain roads.

Chuck Gathers had a girlfriend named Joanne Atanasoff,

who was of Bulgarian extraction and gorgeous. She was one of the two cheerleaders. Dick also had a girlfriend, whose name was Lynn Robinson, and the two couples were close, spending a lot of time together. I seldom saw my brother except when he came home to sleep.

* * *

For spring vacation, there was to be another mountain adventure for the Scouts. Mr. Swerdfeger took six of us up to Camp Tahosa, a small Boy Scout camp at 10,000 feet, a little north of Ward, on a small lake over which cold winds blew most of the time. There were several little cabins with rock walls, and we were assigned to one. This time there was no CU student with us. We were on our own, except for the camp guardians who lived in a comfortable house a little below the lake and out of the heavy cold wind patterns. It was a very cold week for us few Scouts who had been abandoned up there. It was another test of our endurance and cooperation to stay warm and fed.

7

At the top of the Gregory Canyon Trail, a few miles west of Boulder and just behind the First Flatiron, is the Green Mountain Lodge. It was also called the Boy Scout Cabin, as it was available to Scout troops for overnight camping.

It was late spring in 1949 when Jim suggested we all back-pack up the canyon and spend the night at the Boy Scout Cabin. The group consisted of Jim Vickery, Cliff Chittim, John Clark, and me. We were full of anticipation at spending the night out in the spooky old cabin deep in the mountains.

The Gregory Canyon Trail used to be a stagecoach and mail run, and we marveled at how those old wagons had lurched up the steep sections of the middle trail portion, which were basically small cliffs. That was before the roads were built up Flagstaff Mountain and from Boulder Canyon to the West Magnolia mining camps south of Boulder Canyon.

Those cliffs were still covered with snow as we carefully made our way up. The upper bit of the Gregory Canyon Trail is short and pleasant but still had snow on it as we approached the cabin.

The Boy Scout Cabin was a rock-walled single-story structure with a fireplace in the north end. Set in the woods at the top of Gregory Canyon, the cabin was seldom used and left unlocked. We entered and opened a couple of the old wood shutters on the windows on its east side for air. But we left the shutters on the west side closed. Back then we had no air mattresses or soft pads but happily just spread out our sleeping bags on the concrete floor. There was an old picnic table in the south end, where we quickly heated up our canned beef stew dinner on our Primus stoves and ate hungrily as night fell.

Then Jim launched into his latest Old Ed story.

"Old Ed is around here," Jim began. Jim was a natural storyteller. Highly animated, his eyes glistened as he looked at the rest of us. Cliff, John, and I waited in anticipation.

The night had fallen fully, and there was a heavy wind blowing the pine trees back and forth outside. The only light was from our fire in the fireplace. It flickered wildly when a strong gust blew overhead, but the fire did not go out. Smoke added to the dimness of light in the room. The shutters creaked in the wind.

"Where is he now?" asked Cliff, looking out the window into the dark.

"Nobody knows exactly where Old Ed is, anytime!" Jim explained, looking sternly at Cliff. "But Old Ed knows. And he knows we are here. Old Ed knows these mountains, and he knows this cabin."

John looked out the window into the dark where Cliff was looking. It was pitch dark out there. There were no other lights in the trees and hills surrounding the cabin. The wind howled, and the shutters banged incessantly against the rock walls.

John looked at Cliff and asked, "Cliff, do you want to go out there and shut the shutters that the wind is banging around?"

"Why don't you do it?" Cliff asked.

"Someone should do it," John replied.

Just then a fierce wind gust shook the cabin's roof. The shutters slammed hard against the cabin and then were silent. So were we.

"Old Ed must have taken care of it!" Jim exclaimed.

We all were looking intently out the windows into the pitch-black night.

"Probably there are no other humans within miles of us," I said.

"At least," Cliff added.

"Except Old Ed," said Jim.

Again we were all silent. Then Cliff looked at Jim and asked, "Jim, did you say once that Old Ed was born up in Ward?"

"No one is quite sure where Old Ed was born. But he mined silver up in Ward before the veins played out."

"That was a long time ago. The early 1900s or maybe before that," I commented.

"What did Old Ed do when everyone left?" Cliff asked.

"They say he lived by fishing and hunting, but no one is really sure about Old Ed except that he cannot resist old towns and cabins and still comes around at night, creeping silently up on folks," Jim said.

The wind came up again but the shutters did not rattle. We just heard the trees banging against each other and the low roar of the wind.

"It might blow all night," John said.

He got up to stick another piece of wood into the fire. "I think of Old Ed as looking like Rip Van Winkle," he added.

"Has anyone seen him?" Cliff asked.

"No. He is only out at night, dark nights like tonight. The wind does not bother him. An old miner up in Lefthand Canyon told me he saw Old Ed briefly once, and he was lucky to get back into his cabin before anything happened."

"Did he say what Old Ed looked like?" Cliff asked.

"I asked him that," Jim replied. "He couldn't tell me."

We were all quiet, thinking about Old Ed lurking around outside our little rock cabin, waiting for some fool to come out.

8

During the summer of 1949, after eighth grade, I discovered the Boulder group of the Colorado Mountain Club (CMC) and their weekend climbing trips. I attached myself to them through Roy Holubar, who ran a small mountaineering supply store out of his basement at 1215 Grandview Avenue, located on the hill directly above Boulder High School. I wangled small jobs after school, helping Roy wrap mail-order requests for equipment in exchange for some equipment for myself. If Roy was not there, his wife, Alice, welcomed me in to do a little work.

Roy imported most of his mountaineering items from Europe, especially Austria. There were no other mountaineering stores in town.

Holubar Mountaineering did have one competitor locally. Gerald Cunningham, a former 10th Mountain Division soldier, ran a mail-order business from his home near the mountain town of Ward. As I got into more high-peak climbing, the goal became to go as light as possible. I wanted a one-man tent and talked my mother into driving me up to Gerry's shop on the Peak to Peak, just north of Ward. We went inside the small house in the trees not far from the road, and there was Gerry busy on his automatic sewing machine. His wife was there taking care of a small snot-nosed baby. I gave Gerry my tent design, which had vents in both ends. He looked at it and said, "Good! I can make it. Come back in a week."

Gerry Mountain Sports later became famous worldwide, especially his Gerry Pack for carrying infant children. His tents were used on the successful 1953 American Everest Expedition.

Holubar also became well-known and went on to open brick and mortar stores in Colorado and other states. In fact, the Holubar brand still exists today, with a flagship store in New York City.

In the summer of 1949, Roy Holubar invited me to join the CMC for a weekend climb of North Maroon Peak, a rugged 14,012-foot peak over by Aspen.

"Do you think I can do it? I've never been that high!" I inquired.

"Sure, if you can handle the altitude. You never know until you are up there," said Roy.

Although I was only fourteen, I happily signed up for the trip, which was led by Roy, with co-leader Horace B. Van Valkenburg, a patent lawyer who lived in Boulder and commuted to Denver for work. His daughter Holly Van Valkenburg was one of my Uni Hill classmates, but we seldom spoke to each other.

The small Boulder CMC group assembled in two cars on a rainy Saturday morning in Boulder to drive over to Aspen and up to Maroon Lake, where we would camp to get an early start on the climb the next morning.

The Maroon Bells are the most photographed mountains in Colorado. Their purple rocks rising steeply above Maroon Lake are dramatic. They look like transplants from up in the

Canadian Rockies. But their beauty belies their danger. More than a dozen climbers have died on the Bells.

It was still raining the next morning as we started out on the path through wet brush on the north side of the lake. "It's wet, but let's continue on up," Roy stated from the head of the column. "Just be very careful once we get onto the face of the peak." The group persevered, and soon we were on the steep couloir that heads up to join the east ridge of the peak, at about 13,000 feet. There was a lot of loose rock going up and then some delicate footholds on the ridge above. You needed to pick your way up carefully.

At one point on the ridge, I hesitated to put my weight on my foot, as I placed it onto a wet rock for the next step.

"It will hold. Go ahead!" Horace, just below me, enjoined.

"Okay. Thanks." I did not slip off the hold.

Everyone made it up the north peak, including me.

"How do you feel, Gus?" Roy stooped down to ask me as I sat on some summit rocks.

"Great!" I replied. The rain was still coming down, although lightly.

A few of the group assembled to do the short but tricky traverse over to the slightly higher South Maroon Peak, which summits at 14,156 feet. I rose to join them. But Roy and a couple of the others huddled in the rain a few yards from me, and then Roy came over.

"We don't think you should come with us on the traverse. It has some tricky sections and some short rappels. I hope you understand, Gus!"

"I know how to rappel," I replied.

Roy was sympathetic but did not change his mind. I understood his judgment that I did not have enough experience. I did not argue and carefully descended the North Maroon Peak with most of the others in the group. As a youngster on his first 14er, I did not mind the advice. And in going down the way we had come up, we found that all the rocks were slick from the continuing rainfall.

* * *

In addition to his basement mail-order mountaineering store, Roy taught elementary mathematics courses at CU. He was an electrical engineer by education and made a little money on the side doing rural electrification projects for the government on weekends.

Both Roy and Horace became father figures to me. We were never emotionally close, but I did a lot of CMC high mountain climbs with them. Neither Roy nor Horace were rock climbers, but that was not unusual since the CMC was principally doing trips to the high peaks. That was fine with me since my Uni Hill climbing friends and I were heavily into local rock climbing.

Neither Roy nor Horace had sons, and I suppose I was a substitute son of sorts. I got to know Roy well enough to ask him to write reference letters for me when I was a senior at Boulder High. The other trusted and willing letter writer was Oliver Dilsaver, who ran Mountain View Memorial Park, where I sometimes worked.

I didn't give much thought to the fact that my relationship with my own father was distant. Nor did I wonder whether I was seeking substitutes. I certainly did not hold my father out as a role model. Nor did I even think I needed a role model. I seemed to be "comfortable in my skin."

Maybe my role model was Natty Bumppo, the hero in James Fenimore Cooper's *Leatherstocking Tales*. I was struck by him when reading the comic book versions, such as *The Deerslayer*, which we could read for free at a little gas station store back in Manchester.

That summer as a fourteen-year-old, I got a paid job with a milk truck driver to deliver milk and dairy products all the way up to Estes Park and even beyond to the national park lodge at Bear Lake. I would ride my bike down the hill from our house on 24th Street to the Watts-Hardy Dairy on Walnut early in the morning, about 4 a.m., to help load the truck. Then off I would go with the delivery driver. Our route was up the North St. Vrain Canyon to Estes Park and then to Bear Lake, where the National Park Service had a small lodge and dairy bar. We stopped along the way at all the lodges to deliver fresh milk. We put the fresh milk in back on the refrigerator shelves, and the older milk was moved to the front.

The driver/delivery man was a nice fellow who put up with me. He was happy to have my assistance and did not mind when I did not show up on occasion because I was off climbing.

I found it to be an exhausting routine to start so early and then work a whole day. Still, sometimes if we got back early enough in the afternoon, I would bike over to swim in the large Hygienic Ice and Coal Company's indoor swimming pool at 21st and Pearl Streets. Across the street there was an A&W Root Beer drive-in that was hard to pass up after swimming.

When the Boulder CMC scheduled a climb of Longs Peak, the 14,259-foot peak above Estes Park, later that summer, I eagerly signed up. My father surprised me by signing up too. Prior to this, he had shown no interest in mountaineering. He was not in bad shape and had never had any weight problems. But he smoked a lot.

The climb was led by Clyde Martz, a CU law professor. I supposed that my father's intentions were tied to getting to know Martz, an important figure in Boulder.

Several cars of us drove to the trailhead and backpacked several miles up to Jim's Grove, a popular place to camp at timberline. My father did not complain and chatted with several fellow hikers, including Professor Martz. He could not have a cigarette at the camp, but he accepted that.

Early the next morning, after a quick breakfast, we all headed to the base of the peak. The trail cuts across a rocky meadow above tree-line and then switchbacks up to the Boulder Field at about 12,000 feet. From some old hotel ruins, we traveled the usual Cable route that follows fixed cables directly up the steep North Face. The cables provided secure handholds, as the exposure was considerable.

For the most part, my father did alright, although his smoking habit emerged in the form of a regular cough. After a short time at the top, Professor Martz sang out, "Okay, time to head down, my friends. We'll go down a different way, by the Keyhole route."

My father then took me aside and asked if I could carry his small daypack going down. I readily agreed, quite impressed by his having made the summit. I shouldered the two daypacks, one over the other.

The Keyhole route drops down the west side of Longs on steep slabs called the Homestretch and then turns north on ledges called the Narrows. From there it joins the Trough, which is a steep descent down boulders and ledges to a break in the ridge to your right, which is the Keyhole through which you pass to the top of the Boulder Field.

My dad did all right with the Homestretch and Narrows, which are quite exposed and where you must pay attention to your footholds. Then we descended the steeper Trough, where the route is marked by bullseyes painted on the rocks. Finally we passed through the Keyhole and the danger was over. From there it was large boulder-hopping to the base of the Cable route and then a seven-mile trail back to the cars.

At the Keyhole (13,300 feet), my father motioned to me to come over and implored me in a quiet, discreet voice to carry his empty canteen down.

I agreed and put it in his daypack and shouldered the two daypacks again. We made it back to Jim's Grove. My father then dutifully shouldered his backpack to continue the four miles down to the parking lot.

I suspected that my father's stellar effort on Longs Peak was tied to wanting to impress Professor Martz, not because he wanted to bond with me. My father was always fiercely competitive. Back in Iowa, he would go to great lengths to defeat John Whisler and me at Monopoly games. In croquet games in our backyard, he delighted in getting his ball next to one of ours and hitting ours very hard into the rosebushes at the edge of the yard.

After Longs Peak, my father never again went on a mountain climb.

9

One afternoon in mid-July, Jim Vickery called and asked me to come over to his house to meet Cory and Lynn, a climbing pair he had met at Uni Hill.

"Gus, Mamoo thinks we should start our own climbing club. Cory and Lynn are here now, and they want to join too," he said.

"Okay, be right over!"

I hopped on my bike and rode across campus to College Avenue and continued westward. As I pedaled up the steep hill of Eighth Street to the Vickery home, I saw two strong-looking fellows waiting outside with Jim. The dark-haired and more muscular one was Cory Simmons, and the other was his climbing partner, Lynn Ridsdale. Lynn was of medium height, solidly built, and sandy haired.

Cory and Lynn had been one year ahead of us at Uni Hill and were headed to Boulder High in the fall. None in our group had climbed with them before. Cory lived over on 17th Street, just below Baseline Road, while Lynn lived nearby on Ninth Street, two blocks from the Vickerys.

"Hi Gus!" Cory greeted me. Lynn nodded to me. Cory was

short for Corwin. His father was a local contractor, and his mother was a climber of sorts. They both encouraged his climbing habit. Lynn's father ran an awning business, where Lynn often had to help out. My immediate feeling was that they appeared to be a powerful climbing pair.

The sun was hot and there was no cooling breeze.

"You guys should come inside our place!" Jim exclaimed, leading us into his house and down the stairs to his and John's small bedroom.

John and Cliff were already there.

"Pretty cool!" Cory blurted out as he spotted the pitons and a rope hanging off hooks on one wall.

"Thanks," Jim replied. "This can be our clubroom."

"Welcome guys!" Cliff said, introducing himself. "I'm at Uni Hill too, in Jim's class."

With the six of us crowded in the small bedroom, we used the two beds as sofas. The little basement was cool compared to the blazing heat outside.

"Mamoo says she'll help us make arm patches for our climbing club," Jim announced. "She wants us to decide on a name."

"What names do you have so far?" I asked.

"Well, John, Cliff, and I like the name The Summit Club. What do you think of that?"

"That sounds great to me!" Cory exclaimed. Lynn nodded his assent.

They all looked at me.

"I'm all for it!" I agreed.

"John Clark already told me he wants to be in," Jim said.

It was now official: our climbing club, The Summit Club, came into being that day with seven initial members. Later on, George Hall and Bill Fairchild would join. On our entry into Boulder High School, we would add a tenth member,

Skip Greene. Mamoo took the lead on creating our climbing club emblem and soon made small shoulder patches that featured a mountain peak design and were sewn onto our nylon climbing parkas.

"What have you guys been climbing?" Cory wanted to know.

"Mostly on the Flatirons and in the Amphitheatre," Jim replied. "But I'm going to buy a used car soon, probably a Ford. Then we can go up into the high peaks."

"That sounds great!" Cory said. "I can't wait to hop into your car and go!"

"Me too!" Lynn agreed. "We can go up into the Indian Peaks. And on the East Face of Longs Peak too."

"I'll be old enough to drive next year too. My parents told me they would buy me a car," Cory added.

"What have you two been climbing?" Jim asked Cory and Lynn. "The usual local stuff. Run up the Third Flatiron after school. Some more serious stuff on Green Mountain sometimes," Cory answered. He paused and looked around the room at each of us. "You guys ever do any bouldering?"

"What's that?" Cliff asked innocently.

Cory and Lynn looked at each other for a moment, and then Lynn replied, "Cory has been climbing hard routes on boulders and rocks scattered throughout these hills. All first ascents. Then it's a contest to see who else can get up them."

Mamoo called down the stairs, "Does anyone want some lemonade?"

We all ran up the stairs and found chairs around the small dining room table, where Mamoo had set out a pitcher of iced lemonade and tall glasses. As we poured and gulped down the cold liquid, we continued to chatter about what climbs we might attempt. We were all excited at the prospect of challenging ourselves with new climbing goals, both locally and on Colorado's highest peaks. Although we didn't know it yet, the adventures and camaraderie of The Summit Club would sustain us for years to come, carrying us all the way through high school.

* * *

Cory later developed into one of the premier pioneering boulderers of Boulder. He used to carry around a little blue ball that he would squeeze throughout the day at school to strengthen his grip. His pioneering bouldering feats later resulted in a pinnacle on Flagstaff Mountain being named the Corwin Simmons Rock.

Some of us tried to follow Cory onto small boulders on the mesa. A rock called Tomato Rock was just a bit taller than we were. If you stacked a couple of small rocks at the base on the north side, you could find several nice ways to top out. Then it was easy to descend by sliding down its south side.

Most bouldering was on slightly taller rocks or cliff faces, but not so tall that you would be injured if you fell off. Cory had very poor vision and had to wear thick eyeglasses. But this did not hinder his uncanny ability to find tiny holds to scale upward on.

Cory quickly established himself as an integral member of our climbing group. He also became one of my best friends.

Our club's forays into bouldering over time extended into "buildering"—which is free climbing on the exteriors of buildings. At that time, no one else in Boulder was buildering, but the sandstone buildings of the CU campus were irresistible to us. We would put up first ascents on the buildings of Old Main, Macky Auditorium, and Norlin Library. Our buildering was arguably a precursor to today's climbing gyms.

Although it was never a top goal, The Summit Club would

eventually achieve quite a few first ascents around Boulder and beyond. These include The Matron's North Face, Schmoe's Nose on Green Mountain, the West Face of the First Flatiron, the North Chimney of the west pinnacle of the Amphitheatre, the Window South Corner on the East Face of Longs Peak, and the North Face of Mount Meeker.

Our club was quite informal; we were just a group of teenagers bonded together by camaraderie and a shared love of mountain adventure. But we were serious about climbing and were pretty good climbers.

Figure 1: The Gustafson family in 1947, prior to moving to Colorado. Left to right: Karl (author), Dick (brother), Jeannette (mother), and Edwin (father).

Figure 2: Boy Scouts at Ward cabin in the winter of 1948. Front row left: Ross Reasoner; back row second from left: John Clark; front row center: author.

Figure 3: John Clark at Loch Vale in Rocky Mountain National Park, 1949

Figure 4: Plane crash, Mount Navajo, 1949

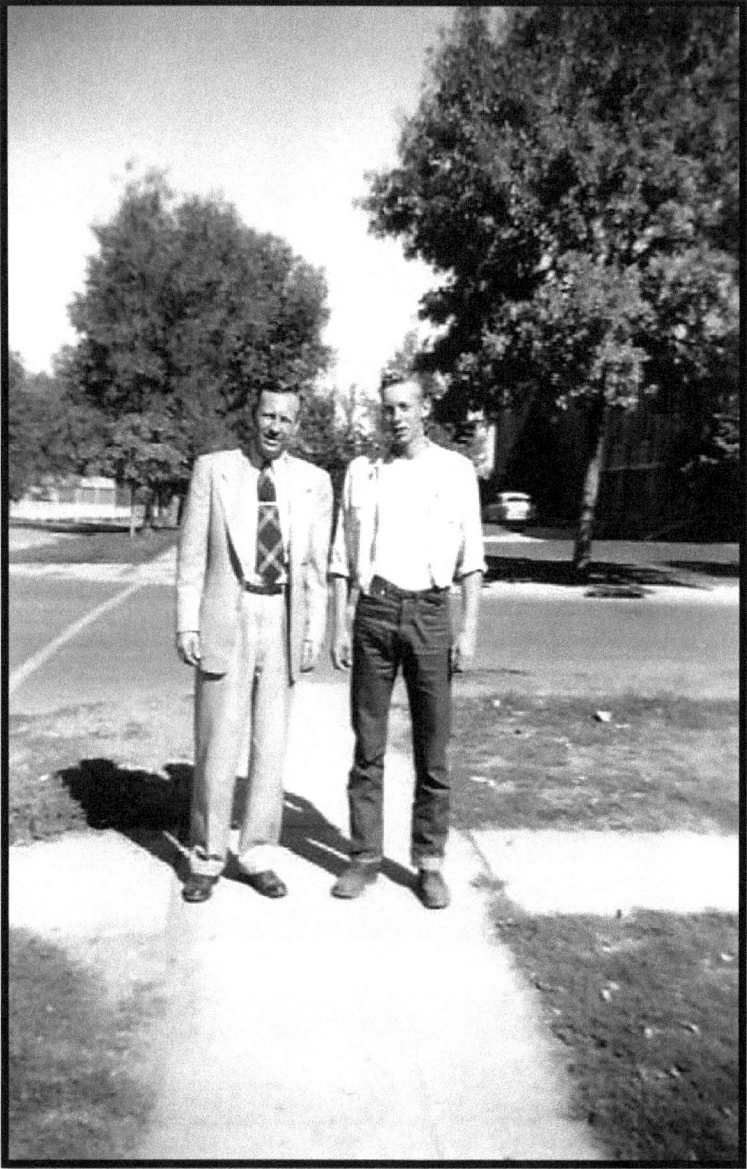

Figure 5: The author and his father in Boulder, 1951

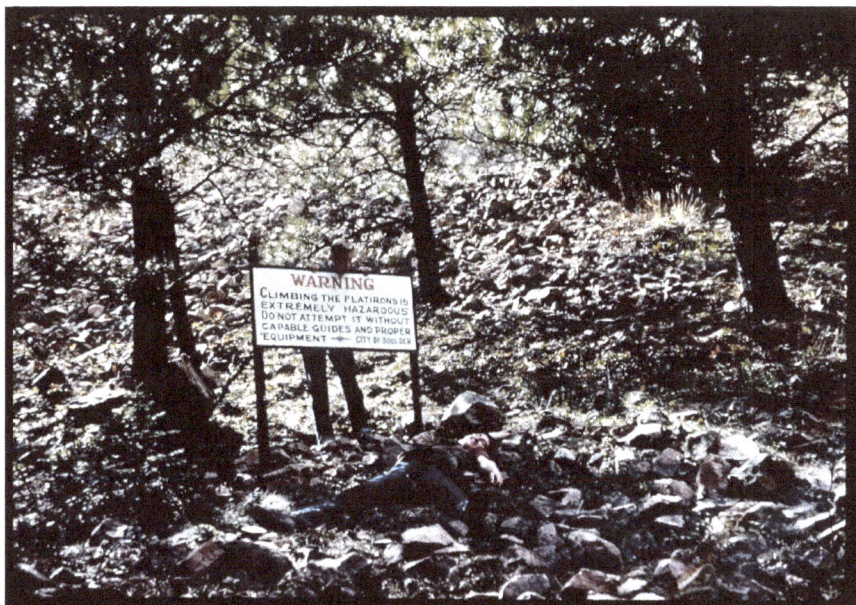

Figure 6: Flatirons sign, 1950. The author is standing; Skip Greene is on the ground.

Figure 7: The author and John Vickery, Kit Carson summit, 1951

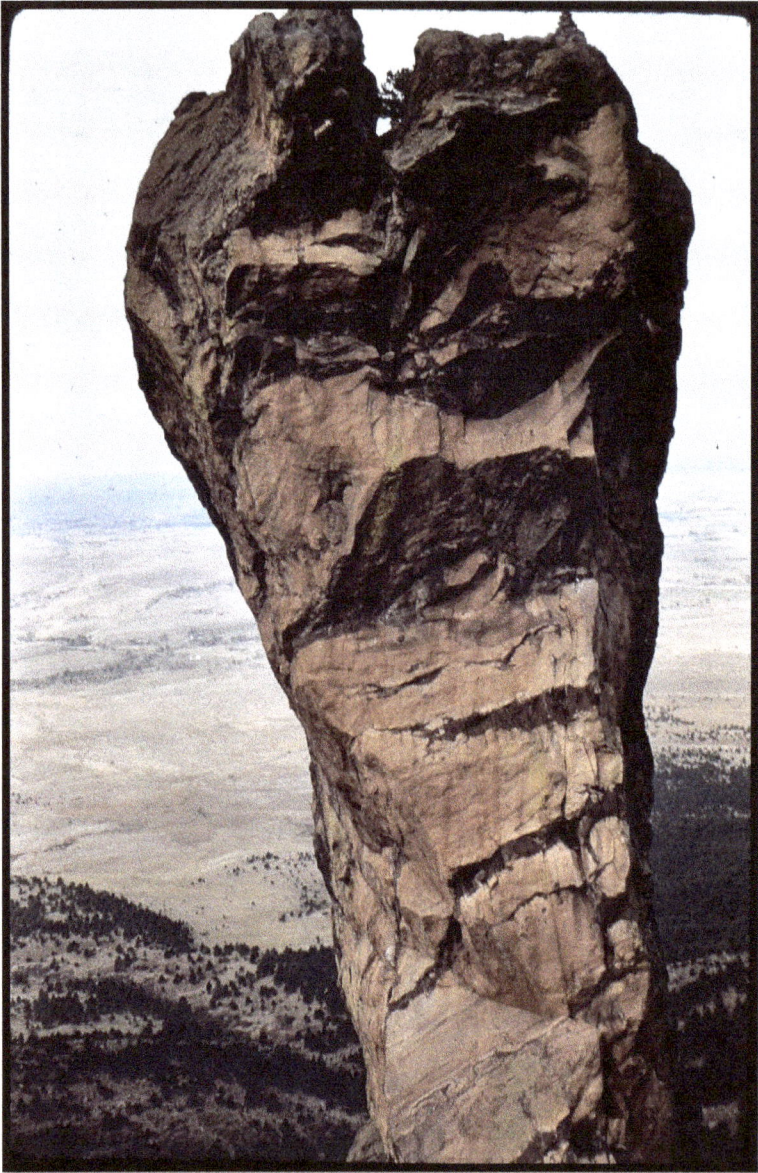

Figure 8: The Maiden, in the Flatirons above Boulder, 1951

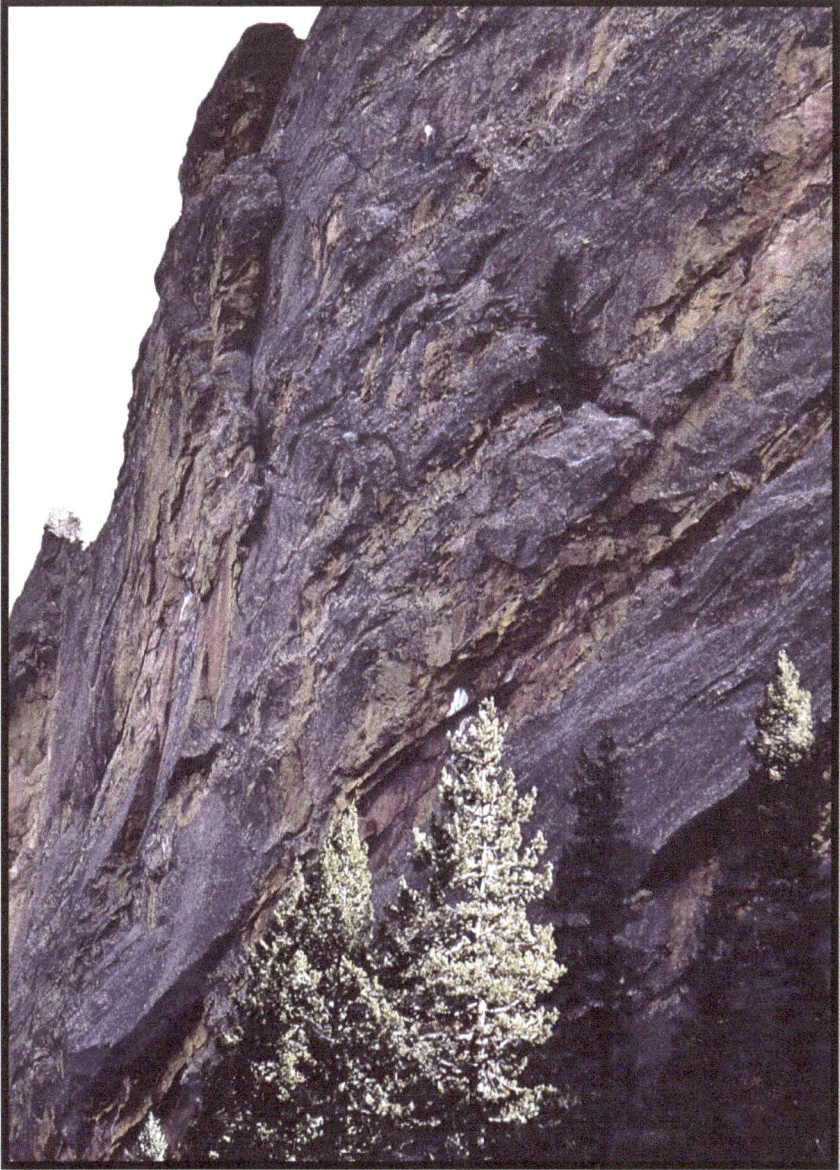

Figure 9: The author climbing The Maiden, 1951

Figure 10: The author rappelling off The Maiden, 1951

Figure 11: The author approaching Capitol Peak on
virgin ridge, 1951

Figure 12: The Summit Club parka with shoulder patch, Capitol Peak cairn, 1951

Figure 13: The author on Mount Snowmass summit, 1951

Figure 14: Arapaho Glacier, chamber of commerce hike led by the author, 1951

Figure 15: Camp at Mount Antero with Jim Vickery, John Clark, and Corwin Simmons, 1952

Figure 16: Mount Antero summit with John Vickery, the author, John Clark, Jim Vickery, and Corwin Simmons, 1952

Figure 17: Left to right: John Vickery, Jim Vickery, and Corwin Simmons on Mount Bross in Army surplus apparel, 1952

Figure 18: Left to right: Skip Greene, Corwin Simmons, John Clark, Jim Vickery, and Cliff Chittim on Castle Peak, 1952

Figure 19: The author enjoying a snack in the Sawatch Range, 1952

Figure 20: The author in his '33 Plymouth in front of a trailer home, 1952

Figure 21: Lynn Risdale in the San Juans, 1952

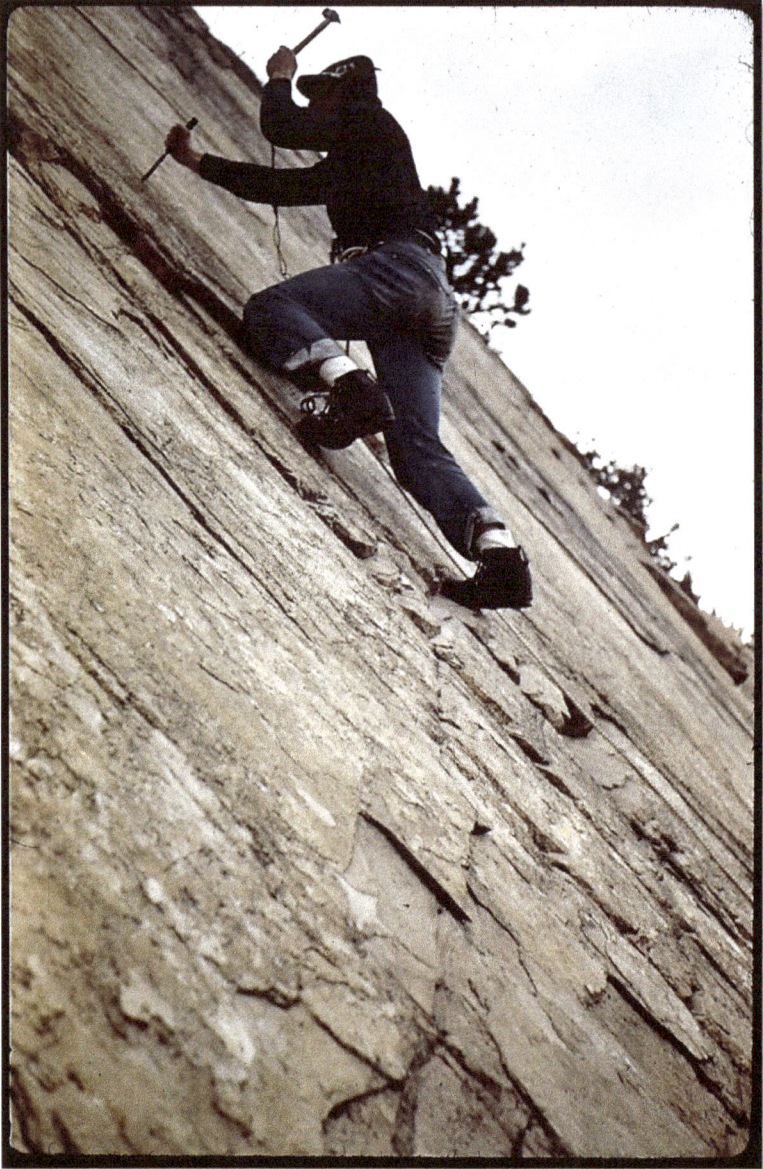

Figure 22: Corwin Simmons on Quarry Wall, practicing drilling bolts, 1952

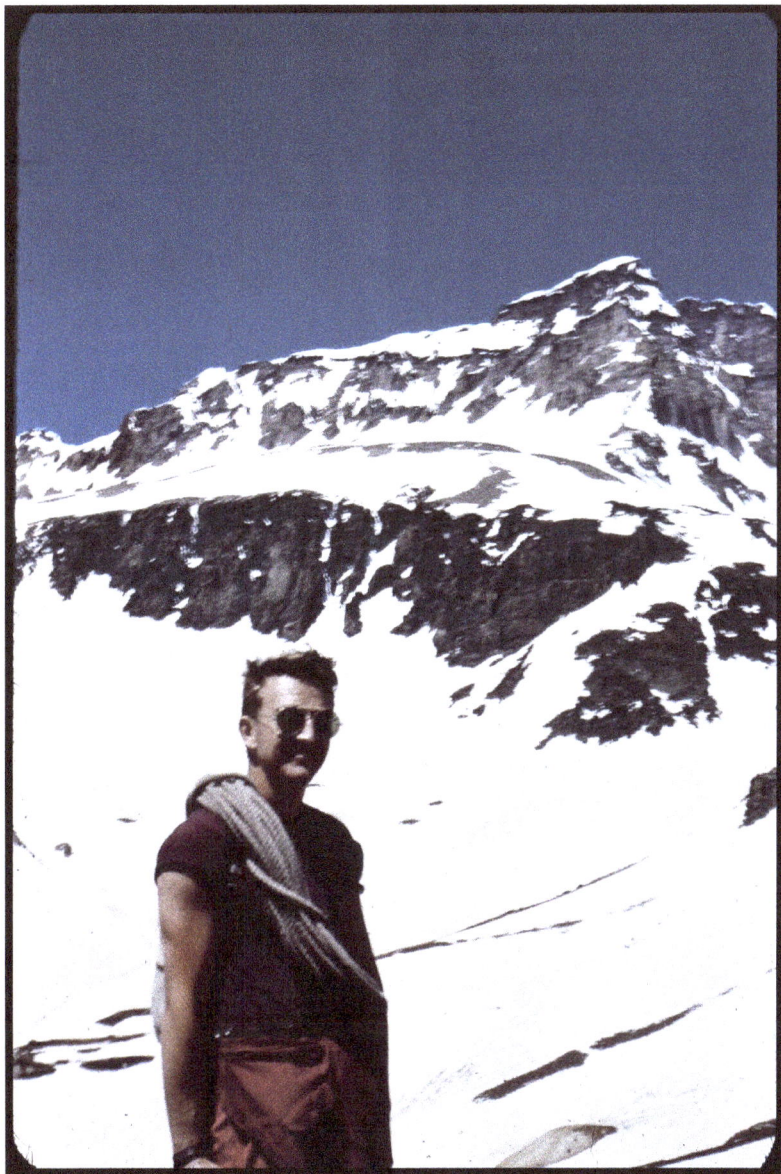

Figure 23: Skip Greene approaching Mount Sneffels, 1952

Figure 24: Skip Greene, Window South Corner, first ascent on Longs Peak, 1953

Figure 25: Jim Vickery at the Great Sand Dunes, 1953

10

"Let's go see the plane crash," Cory suggested one day late in the summer of 1949. We were in the Vickerys' small basement bedroom, and Cory awaited our response.

"I'm all for it!" said Jim.

"Sounds good to me," seconded Jim's brother John. "We could climb Navajo Peak at the same time."

"I think that sounds great!" I concurred.

On January 21, 1948, a Douglas C47 cargo plane had failed to get over the Continental Divide west of Boulder. The plane had impacted with great force the ridge coming off east of Navajo Peak (13,409 feet). The crash site was at 12,900 feet. The impact was said to be so extreme that part of one engine had sailed all the way across the valley onto Isabelle Glacier on the other side. All three humans in the plane had died instantly.

The wreckage was not spotted until May 23, 1948, by an Air National Guard plane. A search and recovery posse from Boulder then set out to recover the bodies. They encountered great difficulty trying to get up there with all the snow. On the north side of the ridge, where the plane wreckage lay, there's a steep gully, with some rock scrambling even if there's no snow. On the south side of the ridge lies the city of Boulder watershed, which normally is closed to the public.

Eventually, with the help of climbers from Rocky Mountain Rescue and a military M29 Weasel, on a final try the team was able to haul the three bodies down.

The four of us—Jim, John, Cory, and I—set out for the crash site the next weekend. Jim was two years older and had his driver's license. Early in the morning, we piled into the 1940 Ford sedan Jim had just bought and headed up to Brainard Lake. Racing up the Long Lake Trail and then the Isabelle Lake Trail and beyond to what some call Upper Isabelle Lake, we paused to munch on some Butterfinger candy bars.

Upper Isabelle Lake is not really a lake. It is instead a delightful little pond of very clear water melting from a large snowbank on its south side. It collects snowmelt from both the Navajo and Isabelle Glaciers. On its north bank is a small grassy section that looks like a planted lawn.

We all sat down on the grass. You could hear the muffled sound of a bubbling brook feeding the little lake. Around us the mountains rose abruptly to the Continental Divide. We were in the Mountain Kingdom.

"I'm for heading up the gully to the crash now," Jim proclaimed after some minutes.

"How far above that is Navajo Peak?" Cory asked. "I want to get to that peak."

"It's about 500 feet vertical. The crash is about 100 feet below the east ridge of Navajo," John explained.

"Let's go," I said, jumping up. It was late enough in the summer that the snow was all gone in the gully leading up to the wreckage. The gully was about 900 feet vertical, steep and mostly boulders, over which we climbed quickly. We were soon at the crumpled fuselage lying there in the rocks on a 50-degree slope. The tail section was mostly intact, and the right wing was crumpled back over the fuselage. The plane was half-buried into the rocks and turned slightly to the right. You could still see the row of windows on the right side. The front of the plane was entirely obliterated, and most of it was missing.

It was a stunning sight.

"Let's go up a bit and take a snack break in a better spot," John suggested.

Just above the wreck, on the ridge, we sat down on some boulders and gazed down on the crumpled plane.

"The search party could not get up that gully in all the snow in May last year," John said. "They had to stay in the bunkhouse at Silver Lake and get up here from the other side."

"There would be a lot of snow on that side too!" I observed. "How did they get up here through all that?"

"They failed for several days," John answered. "Finally they got ahold of two World War II Weasels and managed to drive up the snows to the ridge above the wreckage. Where we are now. They could not believe their eyes. One of the guys leading the search party said, 'It looked as if the very rocks exploded.'"

"What did they do then?" Cory asked.

"Went back down to the bunkhouse and called the Rocky Mountain Rescue Group," John said. "The next day they all went up again and found two bodies and hauled them down. Then they returned the next day and found the third body in the rocks right in the wreckage."

"I might have crawled over right where he was!" Cory exclaimed.

We were silent and just sat there looking at the tragic end of a large airplane and the instant snuffing out of three lives.

"How did it happen?" I asked. "Did they come in too low in the valley to get over the Divide?"

"No," John replied. "They radioed that they were at 14,500 feet but encountering high turbulence."

"People from Kansas don't understand about the downflows coming over the Divide," Jim said.

"They said clouds were just 500 feet below them," John added. "They would not even have seen the peaks 1,000 feet below them in the clouds."

"They might have just descended into the clouds to try to escape the turbulence," I said.

Again we were all silent for a few minutes. It was the first plane crash we had seen.

"Poor guys," John said. "Wiped out in an instant."

"I think Joe Teegarden's brother was in the search party," Jim recalled. Joe was in our class and his brother "Dock" Teegarden was a deputy sheriff.

The weather was holding. There was not much more to say.

You can only look at a plane wreck for a certain amount of time.

"Let's get the peak!" Cory shouted, breaking us free from our reveries.

We quickly climbed west up the ridge and saw that the Navajo summit had a sharp conical top we would have to get up. We found a chimney through the top portion and were soon on top.

"Yippee!" Cory hollered. We all echoed him at once. "Yippeeeee!" rang through the mountaintops.

Looking to the northwest we saw a sharp rock spire rising out of the top of Navajo Glacier. Flat on top where it straddled the Continental Divide, the glacier slopes off east and gets steeper and steeper, with ice appearing more and more through its snow as the summer goes on.

"I wonder if anyone has been up that thumb?" Jim said.

"Really strange the way it just rises up out of the top snow," I observed.

"If you guys will wait, I think Jim and I can get up it pretty fast," said John.

We all descended an easier way down the southwest slopes of Navajo and traversed to the top of the glacier and over to the base of the spire. Jim immediately started climbing, belayed by his brother John. Cory and I roped up to follow. But Jim had found ledges spiraling around the spire and was going up fast.

"Wait a bit, Jim. I will have to circle around with you!" his belayer, John, shouted.

"Okay. It is pretty easy. Just do that," Jim replied.

"Not much of a belay!" John answered. "Don't you want to put in some protection?"

"No, too easy. A bit loose, but I am almost up!" Jim shouted back.

Cory and I circled around with John and just watched as Jim topped out. Rather quickly Jim hollered down, "Hey, guys, there's a can up here with some names of guys who already climbed it."

We were all disappointed, of course, but not surprised.

Cory then called up, "Come on down. I want to explore Isabelle Glacier to see if we can find that engine part that blew way over there."

"Okay. But I will be careful with the loose holds as I come down. Don't leave me here!" Jim cried.

"I'm your brother! I wouldn't leave you!" John joked. We all waited as Jim worked his way back down.

"Leave your ropes on," Cory instructed. "I will lead us across the top part of the glacier to get to the other side about halfway down. Get your ice axes out."

Navajo Glacier is deceptive and had killed many climbers in the past. Starting out from its flat portion on top, it gradually steepens and finishes in a sheet of pure ice, running directly into the steep rocky slopes at its bottom. We had heard plenty of stories about it.

Cory led our rope and John followed, leading the second rope. We took our time, carefully cutting steps, with ice ax belays, moving one at a time on each rope. Soon we were across and on the other side.

"I think we can cut across the cliffs and not have to descend all the way down to the valley and then climb back up again," Cory said. "We can un-rope here."

"Go for it!" John affirmed as we coiled the ropes over our shoulders, as was our custom. We followed Cory as he found his way through the cliffs, always heading north.

We all four could move very fast on ledges and in minor scrambling—almost running.

"*Terra incognita!*" I exclaimed, laughing.

"You just like the sound of that!" said John.

"True. But I don't think many have come across here. Look at all these loose rocks we're going through."

Isabelle Glacier was tucked into the cirque formed by the cliffs of Apache and Shoshoni Peaks, directly across the basin from the airplane gully on Navajo. Our route at about 12,600 feet soon brought us to the middle of the glacier. It was bigger than we had expected. None of us had been there before.

"DC-3s used a Pratt and Whitney engine," said Jim. "Fourteen cylinders, I think."

"If we find it, we will know it is an airplane engine!" countered Cory.

"Let's spread out and look for anything sticking up in the snow," John suggested.

It was like looking for a needle in a haystack. But the weather was good, and we were happy to be on our quest. After about an hour Jim suggested we give up and head down to the Isabelle Glacier Trail, a primitive path winding down through boulders to the Upper Isabelle Lake below.

Just as we were about to step off the snows below the glacier, Cory, who was in the lead, called out excitedly.

"I found something!"

We all ran down the snow to join him. It was a solid chunk of steel about two feet long and a foot and a half deep, and the cylinders looked to be about three inches across. It had been sheared off something bigger.

Cory bent down to lift it and couldn't. He exclaimed, "Wow! This thing is heavy!"

Jim also gave it a try. So did John. Then me. Two of us together could budge it only a bit. It was still frozen into the glacier.

"Too heavy to carry down," Cory concluded. "We might as well just cover it up with some snow and leave it here."

"I'm not sure we would be allowed to take it anyway," observed John.

"If you guys worked on cars more like I do, you would know that engine blocks are very heavy! I almost got crushed when one came loose on me," Jim said.

"Think bars of gold. They are not easy to carry around," I added, laughing.

"If this was gold we would figure out a way to get it down!" John interjected.

We stood there a few minutes looking at the engine remains, marveling that the crash impact could have sent it clear across the valley.

It was getting late in the day. With no more words, we charged down the boulder trail, deeply satisfied with all we had done that day.

11

In September 1949, both Dick and Chuck Gathers enrolled at CU and pledged the ATO Fraternity. Dick still lived at home, but he was seldom around. He took to the partying aspect of fraternity life and did not have any special academic interest. He dreamed of a professional life as an artist and could easily sketch western horse-and-rider panoramas.

I was now in ninth grade at Uni Hill and felt quite comfortable there. I was still a halfback on the lightweight football team, as I was still small. Uni Hill classes were still very easy, and my life centered more and more on rock climbing and my new climbing friends. But as winter approached and the snows covered the local cliffs, our climbing was a bit shut down.

My brother around this time took a night job cleaning the Old Main Building on the CU campus to make some money for his social life. Once he asked me to substitute for him for a week. I went over there in the evening after classes were done and all the professors had gone home. With an oil cloth, my first task was to clean all the blackboards in the building. Then I swept all the floors. The building was not large, and I thought I was doing an adequate job.

But when my brother took over again, he told me there had been complaints. My brother was not an easygoing fellow and was easily annoyed. He thanked me nonetheless and paid me as promised.

Dick and I always got along in a somewhat strange way. Probably he felt a kind of responsibility for me, as he was aware of our parents' shortcomings. I think he tried to fill the gap as a brother.

However, my brother's inner anger and swift temper would haunt him all his life. While he was a good older brother to me, he often erupted at others, including his wife and kids later on. While in college in Tennessee many years later, he lost it at a faculty member during a faculty–graduate student basketball game. He knocked a professor into the bleachers, breaking his jaw. As a result, my brother was asked to leave the program with only a master's degree. Later in his life he managed to complete a PhD elsewhere.

I think that advancing him two grades back in Iowa might have contributed to his anger, as he was always small relative to his classmates. I was always glad that my parents had learned their lesson and did not advance me in my grade or any classes.

Dick always believed that our parents had not wanted him and had married only because my mother became pregnant with him. That was probably true. But many marriages in that era came about that way.

* * *

Like Dick, my father also had a quick temper. He was the sixth of six kids born in the tiny town of Plaza in remote North Dakota. The kids were Clara, Lillian, Anne, Gilbert, Florence, and my dad, Ed. My grandfather Carl Augustus Gustafson and his wife, Sophie, built and ran a large hotel in Plaza, and the girls all had to help run the place. Plaza was a Wild West city at the end of a railroad line.

Ed was a cute kid and was pampered and spoiled by the older sisters. Due to the shortage of male dancing partners in Plaza, my dad was drafted to enter (and win) dancing competitions with his sister Florence, who was five years older. After high school, his father sent him off to a "rich kids" private college, Carleton in Northfield, Minnesota, which did not help. My father always had that "deserving" chip on his shoulder that rich kids sometimes have.

Proud of himself and brimming over with confidence, he was nonetheless a hard worker, determined to succeed. I don't remember any warm feelings between my father and me at all. I'm not sure if my father had any warm feelings for anyone other than himself.

* * *

My mother, for her part, was a bit hapless. A preacher's daughter, she too had been pampered. She had been groomed with twelve years of piano instruction to become a concert pianist. But that plan did not come to fruition. She instead married young and had my brother quickly and later me. She never held a job and developed no career or employment experience, nor any desire for a career after my father left. She would remain restless and unhappy throughout her life.

Because she was pretty, she relied on her looks. Her father, the Reverend Frank Anderson, had first married Anne, the older sister of Clara. But Anne died in childbirth and some weeks later so did the child. The reverend then married Clara, who bore and raised my mother. After so much tragedy, my mother was the apple of their eyes and doted on.

In contrast, her younger sister Leona was a bit homely and had to work for everything in her life. She did not marry until later in life and had no children of her own. She often visited and stayed with the Gustafson family in Iowa, showering my brother and me with expensive gifts, such as cameras, and ready affection.

* * *

I was a determined little fellow, full of joie de vivre but also a bit stoic. It is easier being a second child, and some of the family fury that my brother felt I just do not remember. Rather self-contained, I often disappeared down into our large basement in Iowa, where I had a chemistry set that made hydrogen sulfide, stinking up the whole house. I also had a crystal-based radio set down there. It amazed me when I could tune into Juarez, Mexico. I would sit in our basement for hours and go off into other worlds.

In the cold Iowa winters, my best buddy, Johnny Whisler, and I played pool on the pool table in our basement. Johnny lived just down the alley from me. In the hot summers we played endless Monopoly games over at his house. His mother was more easygoing than mine, and we escaped the heat in their screened porch all day. In fall and spring, we biked out to the little nine-hole golf course that my dad and other local businessmen had constructed. We played a lot of golf.

By the time we'd moved to Boulder, I was used to finding my own entertainment and being largely self-sufficient. I didn't expect anyone at home to dote on me or pay much attention to my life. Since I never had trouble with school, it was always easy for me. My parents really had no reason to complain and were happy to let me go my own way.

I certainly did that from the start in Boulder.

* * *

One day in the fall of 1949, I came home from school and found my brother and my father with neck locks on each other, struggling in the small living room. They stayed on their feet and tried not to crash into my mother's grand piano. It was an almost comical scene.

But they were dead serious and cursing at each other. My mother eventually had to break it up. My brother stalked out of the house, and my father retreated into his little office. I never knew what the fight was about. Nor did I care to know.

As my brother and parents were going through their angst, I did not get involved. A better world was beckoning me: the love and companionship of my band of brothers brought together by climbing. The narcotic of needing to get up there on the peaks. The ache of wanting personal freedom. It was so much fun, pure joy, to go up to the rocks with a buddy and do a climb. The clear air, the view, the whole universe was mine.

Climbing is a bit like a religion. You grow to need it and turn to it to take your mind off the distractions and strains of daily life. I would even call it an addiction, but it's so much more than that, as it nourishes the mind, body, and spirit.

Sometimes I preferred to climb solo. I rode my bike up to the Gregory Canyon parking lot, raced up the steep hill behind the Amphitheatre, and climbed the steep but with many holds west face of the first Amphitheatre spire. Then I carefully squeezed past a small passage that looked down on the vertical Amphitheatre South Face and found myself at the top of the whole rock.

Alone and with all of Boulder mine, just below, I would spend an hour or two up there in a priceless reverie. I then carefully made my way back down and got home before dark.

* * *

My climbing friends and I often got together at their homes and went out on most weekends to do some climbing. We also talked climbing nonstop. That was part of our new world.

The 1945 mountain climbing book *The White Tower* by James Ramsey Ullman (and the movie of the same name, which came out in summer 1950) caught our attention. We knew all the principal characters and referred to them by name when climbing.

"To rest is not to conquer!" the German Hein (played by Lloyd Bridges) said, looking contemptuously at his weakling comrades as they struggled upward. It was 1944 and they were all interned in Switzerland during the Second World War.

Glenn Ford played the American Martin Ordway, a casual fellow whom Hein accused of climbing with his hands in his pockets.

In one scene, near the summit of the unclimbed mountain, Hein is on the final summit ridge, with the American following close behind him. Hein is ahead, spread-eagled on a dangerous snowbank that looks like it could come loose at any time. Danger is in the air.

"Let me give you a hand," Ordway says as he cautiously climbs toward Hein with a rope.

Hein looks at him, pityingly, looks at the steep snow slab, and goes for it.

The slab breaks loose, and Hein falls thousands of feet to his death.

Another of our favorite characters was the Frenchman, Paul DeLambre, played by the French actor Claude Raines. Some might remember him from the movie *Casablanca*, where he plays the French police chief interacting with Humphrey Bogart.

As the climbers make their way slowly up the great mountain, DeLambre is moving even more slowly than the others under a heavy pack. The Swiss guide, played by Oscar Homolka, asks what is making his pack so heavy. DeLambre pulls out a bottle of wine.

"Why are you carrying that thing all the way up this mountain?"

"To celebrate on the summit!" DeLambre proudly exclaims.

"What it we do not make the summit?"

"Then for consolation!"

We loved this movie and felt the characters quite personally. We were much more interested in them and the climbing than in the girl, named Carla, played by Italian actress Alida Valli, even though the book's plot has her organizing the climb, hoping to be the first to summit the mountain, on which her father had perished.

Sometimes on our own climbs up high peaks, if one of us was becoming lazy and not really going for it, another of us would call out: "To rest is not to conquer!" This was a popular refrain by Hein in the movie.

Our buddy would immediately grin and speed up.

12

In June of 1950, North Korea invaded South Korea, and President Truman rather quickly reciprocated by organizing a United Nations defense of South Korea. It was becoming clear to all Americans that World War II had been continued into a Cold War with the Soviet Union.

The Korean War had put an uncertain element into our plans. Nobody wanted to be drafted as a foot soldier and sent over there to die. The fear pervaded our lives throughout our high school years, yet to come.

Ross Reasoner told me one day in the summer of 1950, "I can't wait until I am sixteen and can enlist in the Navy!" Most Americans were naturally very patriotic. I was less so at that age. And I wanted to go on to university after high school, so enlisting was not something I had in mind.

John Vickery would be a senior at Boulder High School the coming year, and he planned to enroll in the US Air Force ROTC at the university. Both Cliff and Bill Fairchild told me they would do the same if the Korean War was still going. I was hesitant to make any plans at all, hoping the war would be won or lost by the time I graduated from high school.

* * *

It was later that summer that the Gustafson family abruptly disintegrated. Although I had known things were tense at home, I didn't really see this coming.

My father suddenly announced that he was divorcing my mother to marry a much younger woman. He had met his wife-to-be while selling insurance down in Vetsville, the Quonset hut student housing for GI Bill World War II veterans. She, Helen, was leaving her veteran husband, who was going to college on the GI Bill.

My father then decided to introduce me to Helen. To facilitate that first meeting, he drove us both up Boulder Canyon to a spot of nice scenery. There we were, with swiftly running Boulder Creek and a canopy of green trees overhead to provide shade. I'm sure he had selected the location to assist with the "sale."

Helen was an attractive young woman. She did her best to befriend me.

"Well, Karl! I'm proud to meet you!"

"A lot of my friends call me Gus," I responded.

"I can call you Gus if you like," she agreed, with a big smile.

I looked over at my dad, who was standing some steps away. He was beaming, more proud of himself than of his new bride-to-be.

"You should be proud of your son, Ed! He is a fine boy."

"You bet!" Ed said, without much feeling.

"Come on over and join us!" Helen commanded.

I felt quite relaxed talking with her. Helen was not self-centered like my father, and she was just doing his bidding for the day. He tried to keep his mouth shut and let her do the talking. But what was I supposed to do or say? Welcome her heartily? My father did his best to sell her to me.

I would say it was a draw. No sale but no repudiation either.

Some weeks after, the two of them ran off to Albuquerque to start their new life together. The marriage culture was like that in those days. The man who was dumping his wife ran off with his new one to another town and started a new job there. Basically, he was dumping his whole previous life, including his two sons.

My father knew that he could start and run any business. He had earned his spurs owning the Gambles store in Manchester, Iowa. His father had given him $3,000 to start that store in the depths of the Great Depression, which was a lot of money in those days. But my father usually took full credit for anything and forgot those who had helped him.

I was not sure if he was running some hardware store in Albuquerque or if he was starting a new life insurance agency there. I never wondered about it or asked.

* * *

Dick, meanwhile, had managed to flunk out of CU in his first year. He then married his high school sweetheart, Lynn, who was the daughter of Boulder High's principal. Lynn was bright and the valedictorian of her class. Clearly Dick and Lynn needed somewhere to live, and he needed a job. Repugnant as it was to him, Dick had no choice but to ask my father for help.

My father contacted the owner of the Gambles store in Albuquerque and managed to get my brother a job there as a claims repossessor. It was dangerous work, and Dick carried a pistol just in case. Then after a few months, my father found him a job as assistant manager of the Gambles store in the small town of Alliance, Nebraska.

Meanwhile, alone in Boulder, my mother panicked over the idea of maintaining our house and its yard, and she sold it quickly. She had gotten the house and some money in the divorce settlement, but she must have realized that the money wouldn't go far.

And she had no idea at all of how to do yard work. She did figure out that I would not be doing much of it. The plot was a full quarter acre, although much of the back was just dirt and a primitive garden I got going to raise strawberries to sell to local markets. All I had to do was water them every few days from the small irrigation ditch that ran through our backyard.

Without any discussion with me, my mother promptly moved us into a 28-foot trailer home in the Joratz Motel and Trailer Court, which sat at 24th and Water Streets in a poor part of Boulder, next to the railroad tracks. I was to sleep in its south end, crammed into a space that held a bed between its walls. My mother would sleep on a sofa on the trailer's north end. In between our respective ends of the trailer were the kitchen, a small table, and a bathroom. There was a separate door to my little bedroom.

There were a few other trailers nearby and a couple of small cinderblock houses that Annie Joratz rented to longer-term visitors. Our trailer sat right next to the houses.

At the north side of the lot were some motel rooms, which Joe Joratz had built and faced with stone. Then he'd had a heart attack, and the running of the place was left to his wife, Annie. She was a forceful woman, active in Democratic politics and not prone to suffer any nonsense. She ran the place like an army sergeant. It was quite secure no matter its neighborhood, which was nearly a slum.

I was not happy with this move.

"Where can I put my climbing and camping gear?" I peremptorily asked my mother.

She looked perturbed. "There is some space under the trailer."

"What if it rains? Snows?"

"Well, it's camping gear, isn't it?"

"I will give it a try," I responded. "Probably I can set the stuff on some wood planks."

A few days after we made the move to the trailer, Jim Vickery pulled up in his 1940 blue Ford. "Gus, old buddy! Want to go for a ride in my car?"

"Sure. What do you think of this trailer home?"

"Gus, old buddy, don't you worry! We'll keep climbing and being buddies together!"

"Thanks Jim. It's not too hard to ride my bike up to your place."

"And you are actually closer to Boulder High School down here!" Jim added.

My other friends were equally supportive. And the Vickerys' small basement bedroom was still our favorite meeting place for The Summit Club.

My mother had quickly sold the little house at 2435 Pennsylvania to my father's business partner, Harl Douglas, the Boulder lawyer who had handled their divorce. This was poor judgment on the part of my mother. A few years later Harl sold it to St. Aidan's Episcopal Church for a good profit. The church rented it out for a few years and then demolished it in 1965 to expand its main chapel.

* * *

Periodically my father would come up to Boulder from Albuquerque and I would have to see him on a weekend day. I didn't mind, although I would rather be out climbing or making money at odd jobs.

One day my father decided to give me driving lessons out at the Mountain View Memorial Park cemetery, in which he was a partner. The cemetery had an oval drive through it and usually no traffic at all. There were two stop signs where roads entered the cemetery.

"When you come to a stop sign, you don't have to stop completely. Just shift into a lower gear and glide on through," he said and proudly showed me how. That gained him a few seconds.

"What if somebody is coming?"

"Well! Then you have to stop!" he shouted exasperatedly, looking at me like I was some kind of dummy.

"I think the driver's license booklet says stop completely first so you can take a good look."

He just grunted and looked at me with marked dissatisfaction and went on to other instructions.

He liked modest Plymouth sedans and was always telling me how smart his policy was to buy a new one every two years, so as to have a prudent image with his customers. Planned obsolescence was just fine.

He had never offered to help me buy a car; nor did I ask.

The driving lessons did not go well, and he soon quit coming up from Albuquerque. I did not see much of him thereafter for years.

* * *

My brother and his young family were secure at least, although poorly paid, running the Gambles store in Alliance, in remote western Nebraska. Their son Chuck, their first child, was born on March 14, 1951.

Lynn's father, Owen Robinson, had by then left Boulder High School to take the high school principal position in Sheridan, Wyoming. The Gambles store in nearby Buffalo, Wyoming, was up for sale, and Dick wanted to move his small family there. My mother then loaned my brother a substantial sum so he could buy and run that store.

Around this time, my mother met a nice guy named Jack Atkinson, a civil engineer working on the new Denver–Boulder Turnpike. Jack was divorced from his first wife, who lived on the Western Slope somewhere with their son.

On weekends my mother and Jack would jump into his pickup truck and go explore the old mountain roads west of Boulder. I was happily left on my own. While my mother still took care of me in a rudimentary way, providing food and shelter, it was clear that her heart was not in it. I did not begrudge her at all.

I felt set free and was ready for it! The mountains welcomed me, and I reciprocated enthusiastically. My new climbing friends became my new family. The mountains became a second home. I felt like a young stallion who had broken free and traveled where and when I wanted.

13

In September of 1950, the rival Casey and Uni Hill ninth-grade classes merged to form the new tenth grade at Boulder High School. Boulder High was then a three-year school, unlike today's four-year format. Still, the school seemed immense to me, physically and with the zillions of students crowding its halls between classes.

Our graduating class in 1953 would have two hundred members. Some kids came to Boulder High from Louisville, Lafayette, Eldorado Springs, and other nearby small towns and mountain hamlets.

My tenth-grade math course, plane geometry, was a wake-up call for me. It was the first time since I had left Iowa that I really had to pay attention to academics. You had to prove new constructions using previously proven constructions. In a sense, it was an introduction to the concept of proof. Our teacher, Mrs. Oliver, was middle aged, tall, and slight of build, which augmented her rather stern visage. She welcomed her new class of about twenty students.

"You won't have to do any homework in this class," Mrs. Oliver announced. "But you must pay close attention to what

I say and not miss any classes."

I looked around the room, and of all my friends, I saw only Cliff Chittim there. The process of filtering the students into the college prep track and "all others" had begun.

The wrestling coach was Allen Patten, who also taught chemistry. I took one quarter of wrestling to fulfil the PE requirement. A small building over by the football field served as the wrestling gym. As your back was on the mat and you were fighting off someone who was trying to pin you, you looked up at the ceiling and saw a big sign saying, "When the Going Gets Tough, the Tough Get Going."

In tenth grade I was still small, but I was strong in a wiry way, and Coach Allen invited me to try out for the wrestling team. But I had no desire to spend my afternoons getting mat burns while fighting for my life.

Tennis was taught by John Fitch. I had played some tennis back in Iowa and had a decent serve. John offered me the chance to try out for the team. Why would I do that? I would much rather be up on the rocks after school.

Biology was taught by Mr. Hamilton. I think he had an advanced degree in the subject. At least once a week he would rant against Wonder Bread.

"Take away sixteen good ingredients and add one! That's a wonder, all right!"

The parents all tolerated him. But they continued to want their pure white slices of bread.

I tried out for the basketball team, since my fondness for the sport remained, but my smallness relegated me to the bench most of the time. After a few weeks I dropped out.

Track was better, and after school I often joined track team workouts. But I would not get competitive until my senior year, when I was much taller and stronger. Besides, if I could be up in the Amphitheatre or on the Flatirons for an afternoon climb, that usually won out.

* * *

My climbing friends from Uni Hill were all at Boulder High now, but the different classes and large numbers of students traveling through the halls between classes overwhelmed our little clique. This was a big-time high school. It was fun for me, since I am basically an extrovert, but I've always had periods of shyness.

One day after school a nondescript fellow ran to catch up with me.

"Hi. I'm Skip Greene. I heard that you were a climber," he said.

His manner of speaking was somewhat self-effacing. But there was confidence underneath.

"Well, great to meet you!" I replied, looking at him expectantly.

"I'm a climber too," he announced. "I learned to do it myself! Do you want to do some climbs together?"

Skip Greene lived in North Boulder in a little house on 4th Street just below Mount Sanitas. There were small rocks about 30-feet high right beside his house, and Skip had taught himself how to self-belay and climb solo, beginning there.

None of us climbers at Uni Hill had ever met Skip. He had attended Casey Junior High, and his climbing had been mostly practiced on the north side of town. Skip, whose real first name was Ralph, like his father, tended be taciturn, almost like an old man. He liked to keep to himself.

But Skip and I soon decided to become regular climbing partners and were extremely compatible. I was rather talkative whereas Skip was a man of few words. He was without question a tough and fearless individual, willing and even driven to try to climb anything. And he did it well.

Skip had gleaned some of his climbing techniques from Harold Walton, a professor of chemistry at the university and a renowned climber. Walton made numerous first ascents of high peaks in the Andes but was also an avid local rock climber. The Waltons lived high up on University Hill. Skip had made friends with the Waltons' daughter and would often go over and chat with Harold about climbing.

* * *

Over Christmas break at the end of 1950, Skip invited me to join him to make a little money. We served as sledding guards for the portion of Ninth Street running downhill from Mapleton Avenue, which the city blocked off after a good snow. It was steep enough for good sledding, but with no runout at the bottom.

Skip and I stood at the intersection of Ninth and Spruce Streets and made sure no cars hit the sledding kids. The bitter cold of December was offset by a big barrel the city provided, into which Skip and I fed wood or anything else that would burn and generate some heat. At the same time, we always watched to catch some errant kid who had gone too fast without braking on their way down.

I was amazed at Skip's hardiness. But the son of a hard-drinking bricklayer father and an underpaid elementary school teacher mother, he needed the money.

"Want to keep doing this through the winter?" Skip asked me as we stood there shivering. "The money is good."

"Yeah, and I can use the money too," I responded, shivering and stomping around near the fire barrel.

"Besides, we can't climb in this kind of weather!" Skip answered as he shoved another piece of wood into the top of the open barrel.

"Wouldn't be any fun, anyway!" I added. I glanced up Ninth Street. It was so cold that only a couple of kids were sledding. They had to pull their sleds to the top of the hill to do another run.

* * *

Skip was one year older than me and had bought an old 1940 Ford sedan. One day in the early spring of 1951, Skip suggested that we drive down to look at The Matron, an angry great fang of a rock that shot up about 1,000 feet from Shadow Canyon, not far from the town of Eldorado Springs, which lies south of Boulder.

"I've heard it has never been climbed, Gus," Skip said, looking directly at me. "I've heard that Dale Johnson and some of the other CU climbers have been looking at it."

"Okay. Let's go!" I said, already excited about the prospect of a new challenge and a possible first ascent. "I'll bring along the new 300-foot rappel rope I just earned at Holubar's."

Skip managed to get his Ford up the old road to a collapsed cabin on the mesa a short distance from Shadow Canyon. In short order we had reached the base of the imposing rock.

It was a bit after noon when we got there. The day was bright and promising.

"I've heard that Dale Johnson is eyeing a route on the south face," Skip offered.

We studied the south face, which was obliquely seen from just below the rock.

"I can see his probable route," I said. "It looks a little loose."

"Let's look at the whole rock," Skip suggested. "It won't

take long."

We headed up the steep slope to the north of The Matron. Right at the bottom of the rock were some funny little troughs that one might squeeze up to access the sheer 60-degree east face of the mighty rock. We both agreed to keep looking.

About halfway up the boulders and brush on the north side of the spire, we made out an attractive possible route heading up the short north face and then curving out onto the long east face. The latter looked like it should be easier climbing, although relying on steep and never-ending friction.

We continued up to circle behind The Matron, which now towered over us as it hung above Shadow Canyon. Descending the slopes on its south face we again passed under Dale Johnson's potential route. At the bottom, having circumnavigated the whole massive spire, we stopped for some water and engaged in the inevitable climbing discussion.

"You said you wanted to just take a look?" I inquired. I suspected correctly that merely taking a look was not in Skip's nature.

"I think we should try that route on the north face," Skip replied without hesitation.

"Fine with me! Let's do it!"

We again made our way up the north slope, which was a jungle of fallen trees and boulders. The climb started out with a classic beautiful layback crack formed by a huge boulder that had fallen against The Matron's north face. Then the route presented two possibilities: an awkward set of little cracks to the right or some smooth little friction cups to the left. We chose the latter route, to the left, and were soon at a little cave and a tree in a crack that led up to the long smooth east face.

I still remember leading up that long face, climbing by friction only, and resisting its impulse to throw you off the massive face.

"Skip! We're not the first to try this!" I yelled down. "There's a little rappel wafer in a crack up here!"

"No problem. Let's get to the top," Skip replied.

We were able to top out, and the feeling was stupendous. You are atop a giant thin spire with nothing but space in all directions around you. It was now late afternoon, and the shadows of the hills were rising up to us. It did not matter whether it was a first ascent of the formation, but it was the first ascent of the route. We felt all the glory of achieving that hard climb, not knowing if it was even possible when we began.

Using my new 300-foot rappel rope, we roped back down the east face to the top of our route on the north face. We then rappelled off the rock just as dark descended upon us.

"Well done, Skip!" I slapped him on his shoulder.

"You too, Gus!" he replied. "That 300-foot rappel rope of yours sure came in handy!"

Feeling quite glorious, we made our way back to his car as darkness descended upon us.

Hearing of our climb, the other members of The Summit Club unanimously voted to bring Skip into the club. Now we were ten.

* * *

Not long after, Skip and I decided to climb another enticing rock spire called The Maiden, in the Flatirons near Boulder. It was not a first ascent, but we planned to attempt an early repeat of the Walton Traverse route, which was named for Skip's climbing mentor, Harold Walton. When I mentioned our plan to Roy Holubar, he volunteered, rather enthusiastically, to take photographs of our climb.

It was a tricky route, with immense exposure, up and across the north face and then culminating in a 100-foot free-hanging rappel off the summit. The entire experience was exhilarating. Not only was our climb a success, but so were Roy's photos, including several images of that breathtaking hanging rappel down to the narrow and exposed saddle called the Crow's Nest.

With our ascent of The Maiden and our recent first ascent of the North Face of The Matron, and an earlier—and easier-- ascent of the Devil's Thumb with John Clark, I now had all three of Boulder's famous pinnacles under my belt.

* * *

In the spring of our sophomore year, Jim and John Vickery approached me one day between classes at Boulder High.

"Gus, what do you think of Minnie and Jake hovering over the main school entrance doors?" Jim asked, making it sound like the first line of joke. Minnie and Jake in fact were a running joke in Boulder and especially at Boulder High.

I laughed in reply.

In 1937 the sculptor Marvin Martin managed to get two of his creations, a rather grotesque and heavily muscled woman and man, mounted in a dominating position directly over the main entrance doors to Boulder High School. These were bas-relief concrete structures meant to symbolize wisdom and strength. The sculptures had been funded with the new school building by the US government during FDR's Depression-era New Deal.

The sculpted pair were also nude, and controversial from the very beginning.

"Do you want to join us tonight and go up and put some clothes on them?" Jim asked.

"This will get you guys famous, for sure!" John joked.

"Only if they catch us!" Jim replied.

I could not resist the temptation. The night was warm and clear. We climbed up an easy wall of the building above the choir room and made our way across the roof to look down on Minnie and Jake. These were the students' names for Minerva, goddess of wisdom, and Jupiter, the god of strength, in Roman mythology. They weighed about five thousand pounds each but were firmly mounted to the building. Both were easily accessible by rappel from the roof.

"Here's a giant jock strap for Jake we made out of old sheets," said Jim.

"And here's a big bra for Minnie!" John added, revealing a similar article of fabric. We had brought ample ropes for rappel. After anchoring them to structures on the roof, we all three dropped the short distance down to Minnie and Jake and attached the coverings to them. It was quite simple using some tape.

As we all three hung there, John asked Jim and me, "How do they look?"

"Can't see. We are too close to them," Jim responded.

"Want to take a picture of them before we go home?" John suggested.

But nobody had brought a camera.

"Should we go out in front of the building and see how they look?" asked Jim.

"I don't think so. We would be just asking to get caught," I replied. The traffic of Arapahoe Avenue passed directly in front of the school, and we could not be sure we would go unnoticed by drivers or even a passing police car.

"Okay. We have done enough. They are more presentable

now!" John announced.

It was an easy hand-over-hand climb back up the ropes to the roof.

We disengaged our ropes, walked over to the way we had come up, and climbed back down. It had only taken us about thirty minutes in total. We were always fast climbers.

The next day we soon found ourselves invited to the office of the Boulder High School principal. His name was Eugene Gullette, and he'd asked several of us climbers to come in to his office for a chat. Principal Gullette had been a school district staff bureaucrat who had worked his way up, and I must say he was a smooth talker.

"I don't mind that you guys did it. It shows great humor. But we have gotten a slew of phone calls already! Now, which of you did it, and when can you take the new clothing off?"

Jim and John and I readily admitted the deed and said we could get the clothes off that night.

All the traffic that day on the busy Arapahoe Avenue slowed to gawk at or admire our artistry. Within Boulder High we were new school heroes.

* * *

Spring vacation in 1951 arrived, and the mountain snows were at their maximum depths. I was over at the Vickerys' house as we tried to work out a plan.

"Let's get Lincoln, Bross, and Democrat Peaks!" John suggested. These were three closely bunched 14ers rising above South Park, which was a two-hour drive from Boulder.

"There's too much snow still," Jim lamented.

"But we can ski in from Alma and find an old cabin up there on the snows to sleep in and then do all three peaks the next day," John countered.

There was no argument to this, and the next day Jim, John, Cory, and I drove over Loveland and Hoosier Passes to Alma, where we skied up Buckskin Gulch to a rickety old mining cabin at 12,500 feet. The cabin still had its roof, although the windows and door were long gone. The floor was still intact in the front room, where old newspapers had been pasted onto the walls as wallpaper.

Our Primus stoves hummed. We warmed up some canned Dinty Moore beef stew and then settled into our sleeping bags on the old wood floor of the cabin. It was cold. No matter, we just wanted to spend the night and get up early and race up all three peaks. The spring snow was hard-packed, and the next day we would all need our ice axes to go on up. We would leave our skis at the old cabin.

The four of us had just seen a movie called *The Thing from Another World*, which featured a monster man buried in the ice in the Arctic and an expedition of human experts seeking to find him.

"I think I heard something out there," Jim said somberly as we tried to get comfortable enough to sleep. We all listened intently. The cabin creaked in the wind, and there was a strange howling sound coming into the cabin from farther up the snowfield.

"I'll go out and look around," Cory said decisively. He put on his parka and boots and cautiously crept out of the old cabin. "I won't use my flashlight in case anything would see it!" he spoke quietly as left.

"Hell, I'm not going to let Cory go out there alone," John declared as he pulled his boots on and prepared to rush out.

"Me neither," I said quietly.

"Well I'm not sitting in here alone!" Jim started pulling on his parka.

Cory was standing outside without having gone far from

the cabin. We all joined him. He was gazing up the valley intently.

The night was clear and a billion stars sparkled overhead. Nobody said anything.

Then Jim, in a whisper, said, "I suppose something could be buried up there somewhere."

John, also in a whisper, offered: "I'm not going up to look for it tonight!"

Cory and I did not say a word. We were all picturing a monster man lying in clear ice still alive from the rocket crash and just waiting for some fools to dig him out. Together we returned quietly to the cabin and soon drifted off to dreams of ice and snow leading to the tops of three 14ers.

The next morning we were in no hurry to leave the primitive shelter of the cabin, but after our usual breakfast of Spam and Grape-Nuts soaked in canned Carnation condensed milk, we were finally bundled up against the cold and set out toward Mount Democrat (14,148 feet), the closest of the three peaks.

"I think we have to go up that east ridge of Democrat," Cory volunteered.

"Right!" John agreed. "It doesn't have much snow but looks okay."

We trundled up Democrat's east ridge.

"Hooray!" Jim shouted as we reached the top.

"Now we have to descend the ridge and plow up that ridge on the other side to get Lincoln," Cory advised.

"Let's go!" I shouted against the wind.

In short order we were at the saddle again and started our trudge up the ridge toward Lincoln. Fairly quickly we were at 14,000 feet and saw before us another sub-peak before Lincoln.

"That's Cameron," Cory advised us as we all gazed at the

14,238-foot peak. "It's too close to Lincoln to get on the 14er list."

We passed over Cameron and Jim shouted, "Hey, look, there's an old miner's cabin just below the top of Lincoln!"

"Right!" John agreed. "We can have a quick lunch there."

"Sounds good," said Cory.

After our lunch on Lincoln, we retraced our steps to Cameron and then headed south to Bross.

"They used to mine right on top of Bross," Jim said when we got there.

"Usually climbers descend by screeing down the west side of Bross to the valley," Cory announced. "I think with everything frozen, we can find some glissades." Cory loved to try to glissade anything. With some good glissades we were soon back to our car again.

14

The summer of 1951 began with my mother urging me to get a job for the summer. I resisted, wanting to climb all summer. Her boyfriend Jack Atkinson then found me a job working on construction of the Denver–Boulder Turnpike. He, as a civil engineer, was a supervisor on that project.

Although I was underage then at sixteen (the official minimum age for that job was eighteen), he bent some rules and I was assigned as a "survey stakes uncoverer" at the top of the Davidson Mesa overlook, above Boulder to the southeast. My job had me running in front of road graders to uncover survey stakes, whose blue tops were at the exact grading height.

It was a tough job. Sometimes the grader driver behind me had to wait while I searched and scratched the dirt surface to uncover the next stake. It was hot and dry on top of the hill out there. And it was grimy work, especially when the wind blew.

Once every hour we could take a water break. For that there were large canvas water bags hanging off the grader. You could taste the blown sand that had slipped into the water, but it did not matter, and we consumed vast quantities of water. I did not particularly like the heat and dust, but I could do the work and the money was good.

The Denver–Boulder Turnpike's entrance to Boulder Valley over Davidson Mesa is quite picturesque and is the first view of Boulder that most people now have driving in. But for my money, I'll take the view from American Legion Hill coming from due east to Boulder Valley. That's how I first saw Boulder in 1948. I immediately fell in love with that viewpoint, and I still think of Boulder that way. I still remember seeing the fruit orchards down below in Boulder Valley and the Arapaho Glacier peering down at you from high above.

After about a month on the turnpike job, Jack informed me that his supervisors had found out my age and asked him to replace me. He looked at me with concern, hoping I wouldn't be disappointed about losing my job. I wasn't.

"Go for it, Jack! Let me go!" I shouted to him beside his pickup truck. "I want to do some climbing anyway!"

* * *

"Let's climb the Crestones!" John Vickery exclaimed excitedly a few days later when we were hanging out in the Vickerys' small bedroom, considering our next climbing exploit. Crestone Peak (14,266 feet) and Crestone Needle (14,203 feet) are linked by a rugged ridge, and you can traverse this to get both of them if you are agile enough.

"That's pretty far away," Jim replied.

The Sangre de Cristo Range is a sliver of high rugged peaks just west of the Wet Mountain Valley and east of the San Luis Valley in southern Colorado. They are beautiful peaks and form a dramatic backdrop when viewed from either side of the range.

For us Boulderites, the Sangre de Cristo Range also connotes the old Spanish culture you can still find in southern Colorado. Many Spanish names still persist there, as far north as the town of Buena Vista in the Arkansas Valley, up near Leadville, and Alma by South Park.

"I noticed that the Denver CMC has a weekend trip down there soon," I said, referring to the Denver CMC chapter. "I can contact them to see if we can go along." I had established links to the CMC through Roy Holubar and had even been appointed representative of The Summit Club to the Boulder CMC. As such, I did not have to pay any dues to anyone.

Jim and John both liked the idea of tagging onto a CMC trip if they did not have to join the club as paying members. None of us knew any of the Denver CMC members.

Horace B. Van Valkenburg of the Boulder CMC was also going on the climb. He signed us up and volunteered to drive us down to the Wet Mountain Valley with the CMC.

From Westcliffe, the drive up the old mining road along South Colony Creek was very rough. Most CMC cars in the caravan were not four-wheel drive, so we soon stopped and parked a short way up the mountain road. We all got out of Horace's car and shouldered our backpacks.

"I could get my 1940 Ford farther up here easily," Jim boasted.

"But you are not driving today!" Horace retorted testily.

After a many mile backpack up the deteriorating road, we reached a nice campout in a meadow near timberline. The next morning we dutifully followed the CMCers up Crestone Needle (14,203 feet), a sharp spire of a 14er. The needle looks harder than it is. The metamorphosed rock holds thousands of little handholds and footholds as you climb up. No one roped up, even though the exposure was significant.

At the top, after a short lunch, the leaders dropped a rappel rope down the north side. "Okay! Those who want to do the traverse over to Crestone Peak are welcome to use this rappel to get started!" the leader stated.

"Can we go first?" John asked politely. John was always a smooth talker.

"Sure," the leader replied.

John, Jim, and I slid quickly down the rope.

"Let's go fast and set a record time!" Jim declared.

"Let's go!" I agreed.

We went fast toward Crestone Peak, almost running over the fourth- and sometimes fifth-class climbing of the clifflike terrain linking the two peaks. The metamorphosed handholds throughout the traverse helped.

As super-confident teenagers we were sure we had left all the CMCers far behind. We never bothered to look back to check and just romped along the west side of the ridge, scrambling wherever necessary. We were like mountain goats on high peaks.

As we topped out on the higher of Crestone Peak's two summits, we turned around and noticed that two Denver CMCers had come along with us on the traverse. We five all summited together. Jim and John and I were quite surprised to find them with us.

"I did not see you guys following us!" John exclaimed.

"We probably followed a slightly different route," one of them answered diplomatically.

We stopped for a snack and then needed to descend Crestone Peak. But how? We did not know.

"How do we get down?" John finally asked of two CMCers.

"Follow us. We go down the north gully of the peak. It's steep but not too bad," the climber replied. He started down without any hesitation.

Following him and his companion, in short order we found ourselves at about 12,500 feet on a plateau north of Crestone Peak that connects to another 14er farther north, Kit Carson Peak, at 14,171 feet.

"We're also going to do Kit Carson and Humboldt today," said Roy Rickus, the other fast CMCer who had led us down the gully off Crestone Peak. "The weather looks good." After Kit Carson Peak, Humboldt at 14,070 feet would be an easy 2,000-foot trail climb at the east end of the plateau.

Jim and John and I looked at each other dumbfounded. Before we could say anything about joining them, Roy turned to us. "We think it would be better if you waited for the rest of the group and descended to camp with them. Or you could start down yourself. I can show you a good gully to continue down on," said Roy.

He had a leadership quality about him and was definite in his instructions to us. We really had no idea of the terrain we were on.

"You guys have a lot of work ahead of you," John replied thoughtfully. "Don't waste your time showing us how to get down. We'll wait for the rest of the group."

It was almost an hour wait for the other CMC group members to join us, a few at a time. Then together it was a relatively straightforward descent down some easy gullies back to our camp.

We had been astounded by and had felt a real admiration for the speed and ambition of Roy and his friend. We had to ask Horace B. Van Valkenburg about Roy.

"He's one of the fastest climbers I have ever known," Horace replied. "He even went fishing this morning before the climb."

* * *

A few weeks later, Horace invited me to join another Denver CMC climb, this time of Little Bear Peak (14,037 feet) and Blanca Peak (14,326 feet). The ridge traverse between them is a mile-long series of minor pinnacles and is considered difficult. The peaks are south of the Crestones.

"I'm all for that! Count me in!" I agreed immediately. Horace volunteered to drive again.

One approached Little Bear from the south from a place called Arrowhead Ranch, which we drove down to on Saturday from Denver. One could pitch a tent there for the night. The slopes of Little Bear Peak rose directly to the north of the ranch. The weather looked good. There were about twenty of us in the climbing party. I did not know any of the Denver CMCers, but Horace knew several of them.

In the morning, as was CMC custom, we all arose before dawn to hopefully avoid afternoon lightning storms. After a quick breakfast we all set out. It was a steady plod of all twenty of us up the south slopes of Little Bear. Everyone in the group seemed to be in good shape. The weather was still perfect.

From the top of Little Bear, one sees a rugged exposed ridge stretching forever north to Blanca Peak. "This ridge is considered the most difficult in Colorado" the leader said. "Does everyone here think they can handle it? We won't rope up if we don't have to."

Everyone nodded their agreement. They all looked very competent, and we set out single file following the leader. The climbing consisted of carefully making our way over or around small towers that constituted the long ridge. We carefully picked our way north to Blanca. The ridge traverse took several hours.

After a few minutes at the top of Blanca Peak, the leader announced, "Okay everyone. Now we reverse and go back the same way. The weather looks good."

"Do you mind if a couple of us drop down one of these gullies and go back by the boulder slopes to the east of the ridge?" Horace asked.

"No problem. But be careful!" the leader replied.

A short distance back along the ridge, Horace got my attention, and we managed to climb down a steep gully onto the boulder field southeast of the ridge. The weather was blue-sky gorgeous, and the sun was still shining hard. There were no signs of thunderstorms heading our way.

Horace set out, heading south on the boulder field just below the ridge. Before he started, I hailed him down. "Horace, do you mind if I drop down a bit farther and find some less steep ground?"

"Sure, go for it," he replied. "See you back at the Arrowhead Ranch."

There I was, all alone on a 14er in terrain I knew nothing about. But I enjoyed immensely finding a nice path lower down through the boulders and eventually into the trees. There was nobody in sight.

Soon I stumbled onto a small encampment. There was a shepherd there with his wife. They were very friendly. Even though I knew a little Spanish, I could not understand their accent and decided maybe it was Basque. They graciously fed me some food from their small camp kitchen.

By then I realized that I had detoured rather far eastward from the Little Bear–Blanca ridge. I told my hosts I had to get going and needed to cut back over some hills to Arrowhead Ranch. But it had been a very pleasant and welcome encounter.

I still remember the feeling of just cutting up and down

hills and finding Arrowhead Ranch by dead reckoning. Horace was already there and we were both ahead of the main group, who were carefully finding their way back along the tedious high ridge.

* * *

Back in Boulder, we gathered once again in the Vickerys' basement bedroom, as was our custom. John said he had an idea for our next climb.

"I think we should head down to the Crestones again and do Kit Carson and Humboldt."

"What's your hurry, John? We were just there," Jim said.

"I'm starting at CU this fall. I don't think I will be doing much climbing for a while," John replied.

We had all been thinking about these two peaks since that day when Roy Rickus and his partner had gone on to bag them after the Crestones.

Jim and I looked at each other. "I can drive!" Jim said.

Early that Saturday we were on our way back to the Sangre de Cristo Range. After we passed through Westcliffe and approached South Colony Lakes Road, Jim said quietly, "I am not going to push my beautiful 1940 Ford too far up that road!"

"You are not so brave now that we are here with it!" his brother John joked. "But I agree."

Jim's decision left us with a six-mile backpack, but nobody complained. Reasonably soon we were camped again at treeline, just below the Crestone Needle.

Sleep was easy as the weather was fine. Early in the morning, after a quick breakfast of Spam and Grape-Nuts, we grabbed our light daypacks and in no time had gone up the gullies to the plateau below Kit Carson Peak.

"Let's just go straight up to save time," John said as he led the way.

We topped out and found ourselves on the eastern false summit of the peak, at almost 14,000 feet.

"No problem. We can just rappel down to the little saddle and go on up the real summit," John declared.

"I don't think we need a rappel," Jim said as he started clambering down toward the little saddle.

John and I followed him, and soon we were all on Kit Carson's summit. The day was perfect.

"Look! It's so clear we can see Mount Blanca down there!" John exclaimed. He was really enjoying his last summit for what would likely be a while.

The Kit Carson summit was indeed delightful, and the weather perfect. We could see very clearly the north gully of Crestone Peak, which we had descended a few weeks earlier.

"I think we should head over and get Humboldt now and then pack out. I can still drive us back to Boulder today!" Jim suggested.

Without further delay we quickly scrambled down the south slopes of Kit Carson, over to the easy climb up Humboldt, and then down its eastern slopes back to our camp. We quickly packed up and set out down the South Colony Lake Trail. It was not very late in the afternoon. We figured it would take us only two hours to return to Jim's car.

We were about halfway down the six-mile trail when John, who was in the lead, suddenly stopped. His mouth was wide open in astonishment as he gazed down the trail, which continued its mild descent between widely spaced pine trees.

"Bear!" he exclaimed. "A really big one!"

Jim and I followed his gaze and saw a giant bear coming straight up the trail toward us. It walked like a polar bear, its front paws slightly turned in, as it climbed steadily and without hesitation directly toward us. Its fur was cinnamon-colored. We had never seen anything like it before.

"That's the biggest bear I have ever seen!" Jim shouted. "Probably near seven hundred pounds!"

With that, Jim ran for a tree to the right of the trail and climbed a little way up its branches with his full pack on. I did the same to the left of the trail. John still stood there in the middle of the trail, transfixed.

Then he quickly looked around and saw that Jim and I had taken to the trees. The great bear continued walking steadily toward him, closing the gap. At that point, John broke his hypnotic staring at the bear and ran to Jim's tree. He could not climb up it with Jim in the way.

"Jim! Get on up there! Go higher!" he pleaded.

"I can't get any higher!" Jim shouted down.

"Jim! I'm your brother! Get on up!"

Jim managed to grab some higher branches. By then the giant bear was on the trail right between us. With ultimate disdain the great bear continued on its way, plodding directly up the trail, not even glancing at us. He was the king of the mountain and knew it. We were peasants, trying desperately to stay out of his way.

After the bear had gone out of sight up the trail, shaken, Jim and I climbed down and joined John.

"We'd better keep going," I suggested.

We continued down the trail, breathing heavily, talking continuously about what we had just experienced. The three of us would always remember that giant.

15

After the Vickery brothers and I had climbed the Crestone group of peaks, I was working one day in Roy Holubar's basement store, packaging up some mail orders. I told Roy how much fun the Crestone and Little-Bear–Blanca traverses had been.

"I think there is one great 14er traverse which has never been done!" Roy mentioned. "And I don't think it would be easy."

"What's that?" I asked, incredulously.

"The Snowmass–Capitol Ridge," he replied.

The only 14er in the Elk Mountain Range I had done was North Maroon, two years earlier with Roy and the CMC.

"I suppose it is pretty loose rock, like all the Elks?" I inquired.

"Not only that, it's long, almost three miles across," Roy replied. "And it's a knife edge."

I said nothing more, but I was intrigued. An untrodden ridge! It was what one dreams about finding as a mountaineer. I did not mention it to my climbing buddies except obliquely, to find out if they had the time and interest to go over there and take a look. None did.

At that time, I still occasionally went to Boy Scout meetings, which were then held in the old Armory Building across University Avenue from Macky Auditorium. The Armory Building had been built in 1915 as the home of the Colorado National Guard, and it still served in that capacity, putting up a few National Guard members. It also had a small basketball court, where some of us would shoot baskets from time to time.

Our assistant scoutmaster was a CU student named Bob Allen. Bob also was in the National Guard and lived in the Armory. Bob liked to hike and climb but had never done any of the 14ers.

Bob also had a car.

"Bob! Do you want to try the Snowmass–Capitol Ridge?" I said to him one evening soon after. "It's never been done."

His ears pricked up. He knew I was deeply into climbing. It was still summer and none of his CU classes had started yet.

"Why not?" he replied.

"Okay! I'll handle the route-finding and climbing gear. Can you handle the food?"

"Sure," he said. "I can gather up some Army K-ration cans for us. And I can drive us over there."

That weekend we were on our way. It was about a four-hour drive to the Roaring Fork Valley. The trail up toward Snowmass (14,079 feet) started at Snowmass Falls Ranch, down at the valley's western edge.

We shouldered our rucksacks and started up. It was about ten miles up to Snowmass Lake. Neither of us had ever been there before. The little I had thought about it had us cutting away from the trail some miles short of Snowmass Lake to get up into Pierre Basin, which lies under the Snowmass–Capitol Ridge.

A steady rain was falling. At about six miles up, I looked at the raging Snowmass Creek and spotted a tree that had fallen across it.

"Let's cross here and head up that slope toward Pierre Basin," I declared. "Pierre Basin lies between Snowmass Peak and Capitol and is entirely above tree-line."

"Sounds good," Bob replied. Bob was a heavy-duty hiker and could be relied upon in rough country.

The crossing was not easy. In fact, it was terrifying. We inched our way across the tree with the raging river below our boots. Once we were across, the slope did not look too steep.

"Let's go up a bit farther until it is dark and then camp there. I doubt that we can make it to Pierre Basin tonight," I said.

"Okay," Bob agreed.

We put in a quick camp at about 12,000 feet, sleeping in the open air with our sleeping bags enfolded in our ponchos as night fell. Our packs were less than thirty pounds, as we had decided to be as light as possible. I had no idea exactly where we were but knew we had to go on up to the ridge far above us to drop into Pierre Basin.

The next morning we were extremely thirsty and searched the little valley where we'd slept until I heard a small stream gurgling. Water! We filled our canteens and enjoyed our last warm meal, cooked over a tiny Sterno can. The day was clear, the rainstorm having passed.

"No choice but to continue on up!" I stated. Bob nodded his agreement.

After some steep climbing up a snow-covered slope, I spotted a break in the ridge above us. We continued up, and as we passed through the gap at 13,400 feet, Pierre Basin opened up in front of us. I could not believe my eyes. The great rocky expanse stretched out, with glimmering blue lakes and snow everywhere, to end abruptly against the walls of "our ridge."

We had arrived at one of the most beautiful sights in the high country of Colorado. It is both the featured cover and frontispiece of the book *100 Years High Up* (Colorado Mountain Club, 2011), although that photo was taken closer to Capitol Peak (14,131 feet). Our viewpoint was across Pierre Basin from a site midway on the preceding ridge.

"Wow! That is a long ridge!" I shouted to Bob. We took our backpacks off and ate a quick lunch of cashews and water.

"Let's get after it," Bob declared as he reshouldered his pack. "We have to cross a lot of boulders to get to that big lake over there."

We made our way down a chimney to the boulder field below and carefully traversed west until we arrived at the lake, the largest in Pierre Basin, lying just under the Snowmass–Capitol Ridge.

"We can camp here on this great little patch of grass on the north side," I said. "Then we still have a little time to scout out a way to get up onto the ridge."

Some reconnaissance revealed that it did not look like we could easily climb up to the ridge near our campsite. The steep walls were all very loose rock that would not support any attempt to climb them. Between the loose-rock walls were some near vertical snowbanks ending up as steep mud couloirs still below the ridge-top.

"We'll go a bit south in the morning and see if we can find another way up onto the ridge," I suggested. "Let's have dinner and enjoy this beautiful spot by this little lake."

A colorful sunset came over the basin. Pierre Basin possesses a certain serenity, being so large and empty, especially

as the sun sets. The weather was fine. No one else was anywhere in the large Pierre Basin.

Rising early the next morning, walking not too far south
over the basin's boulders, we spotted a 1,000-foot snow couloir, which ended about 100 feet below the top of the ridge.
That final near vertical portion was mud covered in loose
rock.

"I think maybe that will go," I ventured. It looked a little
more possible than the couloirs near our campsite.

I led us upward. It was delicate work getting up the final
muddy portion, but by noon we were both sitting on top of
our ridge.

"Let's leave our packs here and go light to get Capitol
Peak!" I cried out excitedly. "I don't think it has ever been
climbed from this ridge."

We made our way quickly north down the loose ridge to
its low point and then started up the next ridge, which be-
comes the South Ridge of Capitol Peak. We had previously
agreed that when crossing the ridge from Capitol to Snowmass, we would stay within 25 feet of its crest. That did not
matter yet as we rushed north toward Capitol. Climbing
swiftly over snow, slabs, and loose rock, we were soon at the
point where the south ridge narrows into a knife edge of loose
rocks, abutting abruptly into Capitol's nearly vertical south
face. The final knife edge was short but dramatic.

"Let me see if I can do it standing up!" I announced to Bob.

Bob took a picture of me balancing on loose rocks atop the
little knife edge. It is one of my favorite 14er photos. And it
was part of a first ascent up Capitol's South Ridge.

Without pausing, as we then raced the approaching night,
we continued scrambling up the South Face of Capitol. When
a rain squall overtook us, we found and ducked into a small
cave to wait it out. There was a small snowbank in the cave,

from which we could grab a few handfuls of snow.

The rain blew over. I found a way to climb out of the cave and on up to Capitol's summit, which was not far above. I was astonished to see that Capitol's summit consisted of little knife edges converging to the high point from all directions.

"Look at this!" I exclaimed. "It really is like a capitol building."

We had to balance along one of these ridges to get to the actual Capitol summit.

"Good work, Bob! This is a fantastic place!"

From the top we could see to the southeast the Maroon Bells, renowned 14ers, rising up not far from Aspen. South of us was our formidable ridge over to Snowmass Peak. It was a spellbinding view.

"We better head back along the ridge soon. It will be dark soon," Bob advised. "Let me take a photo first. Drape your parka with The Summit Club emblem showing over Capitol's summit cairn."

I did so. That photo has an immortal feel to it.

"Okay," I shouted, "we'd better get going now!"

We carefully descended to just above the cave. Then, to quickly and safely get back down to the ridge over to Snowmass Peak, I pounded a secure piton and rigged a rappel over the cave section. Soon we were back down to the little knife edge where the Snowmass ridge abuts Capitol. Without ado we traversed south over the loose rock ridge. At times it returned to a knife edge and was consistently composed of loose rocks. It required great care not to fall off in the dim light of dusk.

Night overtook us as we finally summited the high point on the ridge that I later named Ridge Peak.

From Ridge Peak, in the dark, we descended carefully down steep slopes of loose rock back to the saddle.

"Whew!" Bob exclaimed.

"Me too!" I echoed. "Let's take a five-minute break here."

From the saddle it was a straightforward scramble up the ridge to retrieve our packs. Laying out our sleeping bags on some flat slabs, we tried to sleep.

"Just think, nobody has been here before, Gus," Bob marveled the next morning as we awoke and set out.

"I can see why! So damned loose!"

The traversing of this portion of the ridge was not too bad. As we neared the end of the ridge near Snowmass Mountain in early afternoon, we encountered a barrier set of needles about one hundred yards long. They were strange-looking things, about twice our height, some balanced one against another. They covered the ridge crest.

Meanwhile, a huge rainstorm had been brewing just to the south. By now it had obscured the view of the Maroon Bells in clouds of rain and some lightning. That storm was heading our way.

"Gus, that looks like a nasty rainstorm, and I need to be at work in Boulder tomorrow morning," said Bob. "We should get moving."

"Okay. Just let me make my way through those pinnacles without my pack and then I'll come back."

As our rule had been to stay within 25 feet of the ridge-top, I did not want the pinnacles to change that. I was still hoping the storm might swerve away from us, but that was a forlorn wish. Dark clouds swirled around with the promise of lots of electricity within.

"I will try to be fast!" I told Bob.

"I'll stay here," Bob replied.

It was fun finding my way through the pinnacles.

"It's coming!" Bob shouted.

"Let me get through this last big pinnacle and then I will

come back and rig a rappel to get us off this ridge!" I shouted to Bob.

We were able to get off the exposed ridge just as the rainstorm hit. Walking a long way on snowbanks in Pierre Basin on the north side of Snowmass Peak and then down a game trail by the steep Copper Falls, we found a fallen log across the still-raging Snowmass Creek. Night and the continuous rain overtook us as we plodded down the trail toward the car. That same night Bob drove us back to Boulder.

Some days later I reported our success to Roy Holubar.

"You have to write it up for *Trail and Timberline!*" Roy declared. "All of the CMC folks will want to know." *Trail and Timberline* was the official CMC statewide quarterly magazine. "You and Bob have established a new high 14er ridge traverse!"

"Okay. I will give it a try. Will you send it to them for me?"

"Of course. But I want you to write it. It will be good practice for you," Roy stated.

I quickly wrote an account of our first ascent traverse of the high ridge. It was the first article I had ever authored. I was just sixteen.

Roy forwarded it to the CMC with no changes. They published it under the headline "The Snowmass–Capitol Ridge" (*Trail and Timberline* 404, August 1952).

For me, the Snowmass–Capitol Ridge was a beautiful first ascent of a classical high ridge between two 14,000-foot peaks. But it would be hard to recommend to general climbers. It's much too loose. And the looseness you find in the Elk Mountain Range does not clear itself with gardening by subsequent climbing groups. It seems to be endemic at all strata in the peaks.

16

L ater in the summer of 1951, I was approached by Francis "Franny" Reich, who was head of the Boulder Chamber of Commerce, asking if I wanted to make a little money guiding the chamber's annual promotional hike. This three-mile hike climbs a good trail from the Fourth of July Campground west of Boulder at 10,100 feet up to almost 13,000 feet, reaching the Arapaho Glacier overlook. The summer tourists loved it.

"How did you find me?" I asked Franny.

"Oh, I get around!" Franny replied noncommittally.

Reich was a go-getter who was committed to promoting growth in Boulder by bringing in new businesses and new people. Tourism helped accomplish both goals. In late 1948, he had brought in *Esquire* magazine and 180 new jobs to Boulder by convincing Boulder businessmen to buy land, construct a building, and then loan it to *Esquire* with a generous amount of time to pay off the mortgage.

He was dubbed "Mr. Chamber" and served as chamber president for thirty-nine years.

In the fall of 1949, Reich became a Boulder hero again by

entering and winning a national competition to bring the NBS Radio Propagation Laboratory to Boulder. The same gambit paid off. Boulder businessmen bought some farmland south of Boulder and promised it to the government for the laboratory.

That inspiration of Franny Reich changed Boulder forever. Other federal government laboratories soon chose to locate here. They often used the argument that they could hire scientists for the Boulder labs at lower GS grades (and hence lower pay) because Boulder is so beautiful with its mountains and sunny climate.

"Gus, we've heard that you are quite a proficient mountain climber," he told me in 1951. "We'd like you to guide our Chamber of Commerce tourist hike up to the Arapaho Glacier. We'll even give you money to hire a few assistants too."

How could I say no?

"Sure," I agreed. "That's late enough in the summer that the snow should have melted off the trail all the way up." I added, "But you should hire the assistants," knowing that my climbing buddies all had jobs or other plans.

About two hundred folks signed up for the annual hike, and their cars filled and overflowed from the little parking lot at the Fourth of July Campground. After a hearty western breakfast of eggs and pancakes prepared by chamber volunteers, Franny caught my attention and called out, "Time to go, right, Gus?"

"Right." I was little concerned because clouds had been building in the west over Arapaho Peak, but I didn't mention it, wanting to appear cool and confident.

Standing in a prominent place above the crowd, I shouted out loudly to the crowd: "Hi ho! Let's go!"

The hikers assembled obediently single-file on the narrow

trail that climbs up out of the campground and turns west toward Arapaho Pass. The Glacier Overlook Trail would branch off two miles up. A few assistants hired by Franny had interspersed themselves into the line.

The Arapaho Pass Trail is very pretty, with many wildflowers, and the group often stopped to admire them.

"No picking flowers!" I admonished them. "Hi ho. Let's go!"

The vibe felt good, and everyone seemed to enjoy my playing the role of mountain guide. Above all, they were all eager to see the glacier.

Soon we were at the old Fourth of July Mine site at timberline. Here the Glacier Overlook Trail branches off to climb north toward an overlook on a ridge just east of South Arapaho Peak.

At this point I instructed my assistant guides, "If anyone is too tired to go up this next slope of switchbacks, tell them to head down now before the rain comes! They can return down this simple trail." One assistant then volunteered to lead them, if need be.

"Hi ho! Let's go!" I shouted out again as we started up the switchbacks toward the overlook. I set a prudent but consistent pace, hoping to beat the coming rainstorm as we headed up.

Once we reached the overlook, the view down onto the glacier would be tremendous. The glacier sits in a large self-carved cirque, above which is the dramatic South Arapaho–North Arapaho ridge. It is a technical traverse I had already made once with John Clark.

Fortunately we reached the saddle before the rain started. Everyone was very pleased with themselves having made it there. For most of the group it was the first glacier they had ever seen.

"Congratulations to everyone! You made it!" I announced ceremoniously.

But I had had no experience yet in my life with crowd control. One exuberant member of the group flung himself into a body slide down a snow slope, heading down to the glacier. "Let's go," he cried, and immediately about twenty others could not contain themselves and flung themselves after him.

I watched with building consternation. What to do?

Franny appeared at the crest of the saddle. He also saw the chaotic tumbling of the sliders, some of whom had lost control. Some did forward summersaults and finished the slide on their bellies, with hands thrust forward until they glided to a halt at the bottom, where the glacier leveled out.

He shouted out to the watching crowd at the saddle, "Please! Please, do not go down there! That is Boulder's water supply!"

They obeyed. Besides, the tumbling of some of the sliders had terrified those watching from above. Franny then turned to me.

"Gus, you better go down there and get those folks back up here. I think the storm is about to start."

"Will do!" I responded. I grabbed my ice ax and started a standing glissade down, executing graceful ski turns back and forth as I descended. The watching crowd at the saddle clapped and shouted their applause.

The group who had slid down looked confused about what to do next. Luckily no one was injured. They assembled around me.

"Franny says we should all climb back up as fast as we can. You're not allowed to be down here," I said with as much authority as a sixteen-year-old could muster. "That rainstorm is also about to hit us!"

Just then a few brave souls who had ventured from the

saddle to the South Arapaho Peak Trail knocked some tire-size boulders, which came bouncing down the snows toward us from the ridge crest on which the trail climbs.

"Watch out, everybody! There are boulders bombing down toward us!" I shouted.

They all looked up with fear in their eyes. Every mountain climber is aware of rockfall danger, but for these folks it was a new thing.

The missiles bounded toward us, but the slope took them to our right.

The storm chose that moment to unleash itself with hail and wind. As mountain storms often do, it had saved its intensity for that moment.

"Hi ho, everyone!" I called out. "Stick with me and I'll get you back up to the saddle."

To return everyone to safety, a couple of assistant guides and I had to string up ropes to get people back up the icy slopes to the overlook. With the cold rain already soaking us through, no one needed any further convincing.

The hikers who had stayed obediently on top had already started down the Overlook Trail, led by the other assistants. We could see them in the switchbacks of the trail below.

We were all soaked and cold when we made it back up to the saddle. My admiration for Franny only increased as I found he had waited alone on top, as the wind howled and the rain pelted us.

"Good work, Gus! Now let's get out of here!" Franny exclaimed and plunged down the trail in the lead.

"Hi ho! Let's go!" I hollered as we all rushed down the trail after Franny. Soon we had caught up with the full crowd.

For all, it was a day to remember.

17

The fall of 1951 arrived, and John Vickery was now enrolled at the University of Colorado. Although he still slept at home in the little bedroom he shared with Jim, John was now seldom home. As Dick had done, John pledged the ATO Fraternity. We missed John's natural climbing leadership and calm enthusiasm.

Cory's parents had bought him a small Willys station wagon so he could rack up more 14,000-foot peaks in his pursuit to climb all of them. He called me one late fall day.

"Want to hop into my station wagon and drive over to Buena Vista and climb Yale?"

"You bet!" I answered. "You haven't gotten that one yet?"

"Nope. I will be by your place tomorrow around noon."

We drove over Loveland Pass and then down to Leadville and Buena Vista. Then we drove up a dirt road south of Yale (14,196 feet) to about 11,000 feet. We both got out and looked at the mountains around us. New snow covered the whole Sawatch Range.

"We'll turn in at dark and get up early and have at it!" Cory exclaimed.

"You bet!" I agreed.

We slept in his station wagon that night and set out early the next morning to plow up the slopes from west of the peak. Cory was not easily deterred and set a mean pace. The snow was soon more than a foot deep, and we had no idea if we were on a trail underneath it. The slope got much steeper, but I kept up as Cory charged upward.

Maybe the snow made the footing easier. Then we were on top. A quick candy bar, and Cory launched into a descent, following our footsteps up. We were then quickly back at the car. Cory was so strong that nothing stopped him.

* * *

We all still climbed in mountaineering ski boots with Vibram soles at that time. They are good on crags but not so good on the friction climbing one often encounters on the rocks and cliffs near Boulder.

I asked Roy one day if there might be a better kind of boot for just friction climbing. He replied immediately that the European climbers used a *kluttershoe*, which was very light, with soft rubber soles. He did not carry them in his mail-order business.

There was a traditional shoe repair shop in Boulder called Perry's Shoe Shop. One afternoon I went down there with a cheap pair of work shoes that still offered good ankle support. I knew that the owner, Warren, had a good reputation for re-soling climbing boots.

"Warren! I think I have a good idea!"

Warren looked up from one of his machines curiously. He was an interesting guy who seemed to be half-asleep as he talked to you. There was a rumor that he had caught "Colorado sleeping sickness" (encephalitis) from mosquito bites up in the mountains.

"Do you have some nice lug soles, softer than Vibrams, you could put on these work shoes?" I asked.

He grasped one of my work shoes, flexed it a bit, paused, and then replied: "Sure, Gus. Your work boots have a medium flex, not as stiff as your mountaineering ski boots but not bad. I think you have a nice idea."

I was very happy with my cheap new rock-climbing boots. On snowy high peaks, I would revert back to the customary Vibram-soled mountaineering boots.

* * *

By then, I had finally grown tall. My spurt upward had begun in 1950, and the photographs of the Arapaho Glacier hike given to me by Franny Reich in 1951 show a six-foot-tall, well-developed young man leading the hike.

Coach Merle Lefferdink asked me one day, "Gus! Do you want to be on the varsity basketball squad?"

"Okay, thanks, I will give it a try."

I was finally big enough and could shoot quite well. But I did not have any real aggression in my bones. I just could not see getting in there and fighting for the ball. I played as a reserve in a few games. I would alternate between practicing with the varsity squad and playing some intramural ball on a team in the evenings. I figured one would help the other.

Merle was quite a good recruiter and coached both the football and basketball teams. He favored his football players on the basketball team but tolerated my splitting my time between basketball and climbing.

* * *

Algebra 1, the next course in the mathematics sequence, was taught by Mr. Saunders. He was very old and would come into the classroom and without saying anything, sit down at his desk, and start reading aloud from the textbook. I did not mind.

The sifting of college-bound students and the others continued. Cliff was able to do the algebra problems, and we could discuss the class together. Neither Cliff nor I had any dreams of being mathematical geniuses. The big thing was to be good enough to get admitted to an engineering school.

Physics was taught by Glenn Gilbert. It was pretty much by the book. Being naturally good at math helped me clear some hurdles. Beginning physics in high school is taught mostly at the conceptual level, so a good imagination also helps. Cliff was in there too, but he did not have the easy time I had.

There were several different history teachers. American history was taught by Mrs. Thomson. Unlike my only previous history course, back in the third grade in Iowa, which meant memorizing dates to pass exams, this course was actually interesting. Mrs. Thomson would often ask us our opinions about various crises and how they had been dealt with.

All my courses seemed easy enough, and I never did any homework. Even in the mathematics and physics courses, I did not have to do homework. The teachers did not demand it, and doing well on exams was sufficient.

* * *

Fashion reared its undeniable head at Boulder High as a cowboy culture hit the school. Everybody had to wear cowboy boots. The idea was to appear to be a good horseman to fit in. First you had to dress the part. Then you had to go out and ride horses.

You could buy cowboy boots anywhere in Boulder. One favorite store was Starr's Clothing Company, downtown on Pearl Street. Starr's was founded in 1914 by a Polish family and would endure for more than 100 years. It became the place to go to buy your blue jeans, usually of the Levi brand. Then you had to purchase a pair of cowboy boots. These would be high-heeled, with a fashionable stitching design inscribed on the sides of the boots.

Some folks would buy several pairs of such boots, especially the girls. Most guys like me just wanted one pair, hopefully a bit scruffy, making you look like an authentic cowboy.

My mother was ahead of the crowd. She had taken up the cowboy culture not long after we came to Boulder. Just a couple of blocks south of our house on 24th Street was the University of Colorado Riding Academy. It was run then by Glenn Grey and offered course credit for physical education at the university. My mother quickly got to know Glenn Grey and joined some of the group three-day pack trips he led over the Continental Divide. This was as she was trying to build a new life after my father's abrupt departure.

* * *

"Want to go riding out north?" one of my young cowboy friends asked me one day.

"Sure! Can you drive?" I answered.

There was a ranch north of Boulder that rented dude horses. We'd rent them for an hour and ride north. There were some old dirt roads you could follow. Badgers and rattlesnakes were sometimes encountered. The snakes slithered off the road, but the badgers stubbornly stood there by their dens or disappeared down them. The horses were not afraid of the snakes but would rear up terrified by the sight of a badger. We would get them under control and detour around the badger.

Walk, trot, canter, gallop, run: how fast could you get your horse to go? Many were old quarter horses that did not want to run any harder than required. We all had spurs, but they were ignored by the horses. Besides, who wants to torture an old horse?

The lope, or canter, was my favorite gait. It was comfortable in the saddle, and the horses seemed to enjoy it too. It was always easy to get into a canter as one turned the horse around to go back to the barn.

* * *

My mother was still stuck with me and that was okay, but she was eager to move up to Buffalo, Wyoming, where my brother's family was deeply embedded in a natural way in western and cowboy culture. Dick absolutely loved it there. For a change, he fit in.

He could ride like a cowpoke and sketch in a few minutes a western scene that would rival Charles Marion Russell. He truly had an exceptional talent that he could have parlayed as a commercial artist. But he had figured out by then that it would not nearly pay for raising a family. His second son, Karl, had followed his first son into this world. Dick integrated himself into Buffalo's town culture by teaching the local 4-H boys club. Meanwhile, he put in fourteen-hour days running the small Gambles store by himself.

I took a bus alone from Boulder up to Buffalo at Thanksgiving break. Trailways had many such short-haul routes in the western United States. I did not have a car yet.

I found Buffalo to be a lovely still-western town. My

brother and his wife and young sons were happy there.

A day after I arrived, Dick took me out with a crowd of local folks to follow a herd of deer up a valley just out of town. We were each supposed to shoot a deer. You could shoot enough deer just outside of town to never have to buy meat in the grocery store. Most Buffalo families did just that.

"Shoot! Aim at one's head!" Dick shouted as we closed on the deer herd.

I focused on one deer and pulled the trigger. The deer fell down. We strode up to it to take a look. It lay there, still twitching.

"Thanks, Dick. But I did not enjoy that. You can have the meat."

"I know what you mean," he replied. "But there are so many deer that we have to clear a lot of them out this way. Some guys just come up here with a six-shooter pistol!"

* * *

Being cooped up in the small bedroom in the south end of the trailer did not offer much to a rambunctious teenager, so my mother would lend me her new Oldsmobile 88 car to go see my friends. Usually I would end up over at the Vickery house, where we always talked climbing.

Sometimes I would drop by Tom Baird's house on Ninth Street, and he would join me for a drive in my mother's Olds 88. Although Tom Baird was not a climber, we had become friends on the Boulder High track team. Tom encouraged me to pick him up at his house so that we could cruise around Boulder for the evening. Tom had moved to Boulder from Colorado Springs for his junior year. His father was pastor of some church.

Tom and I would debate philosophy all evening. He was

a diehard Christian. I, on the other hand, was uncertain, thanks in part to an unresolvable dispute between my Baptist mother and my Lutheran father, whereby I had been sent to the Congregational church back in Iowa as a form of compromise. There the religious training was extremely mild. We kids had to memorize some kind of catechism, but that was all.

I never could understand the concept of blind faith. It was okay to have faith and beliefs and hope they were true. But I found myself generally evolving into a habit of formulating three possible outcomes on almost any question: true, false, and some other answer. I was always comforted by the possibility of some answer beyond us. Believers like Tom wanted a definite yes or no outcome to everything.

Tom was steadfast in his position in our debates but not angry. I was just as steadfast and not angry. We were quite compatible.

One evening I told him about the religious adventure that I had engaged in with Ross Reasoner and Dick Shepherd the first year after I'd moved to Boulder. Dick Shepherd was also in eighth grade at Uni Hill then. His family of many children lived in a small house on 24th Street, not far from our house.

One day the three of us neighbor boys decided to visit every church in Boulder on successive Sundays. I don't know whose idea it was. We dressed up and looked presentable. Boulder was small enough that we could walk to all its churches.

The first church we visited was the Congregational church downtown at Broadway and Pine Street. I was nominally a member there. The next one was nearby, a Trinity Lutheran church. Eventually we went to every church. We were quite proud of ourselves for our initiative.

Tom was quite baffled by this story.

"Gus! Did you three prefer one church over the others?"

"No."

"Well, what did you and they think?"

"Well, Dick actually found a pressed shirt to wear, and Ross and I tried to find clean clothes each Sunday. Remember that Ross was a farm boy and Dick Shepherd came from a pretty rough family!"

"But what did they think?" Tom repeated his question.

"I don't really know, Tom. We all enjoyed the good weather and meeting nice people."

Tom paused, at a total loss to understand. Then he asked me, "What were the different sermons like?"

I could not remember them. But I assured him that they all had a common theme: Be good to your neighbors and your family.

When Tom and I tired of our debates we would drive downtown and get large malted milks at the Alba dairy store on Broadway, just north of Pearl Street. Some of our high school classmate girls worked there. We were served the malt glasses and also the metal mixing containers in which they had been made. You could get almost a full second malt glass from the extra container.

* * *

In December of 1951, Cory approached me and said The Summit Club should emulate the AdAmAn Club of Colorado Springs, which always climbed Pikes Peak (14,155 feet) on December 30–31 and shot off fireworks on New Year's Eve. That sounded good to me. His plan was to go up not for New Year's but during the following week, in early January, while still on Christmas vacation. We would not shoot off fireworks but would just enjoy the winter climbing of the peak. None of us had yet been up Pikes Peak, which we regarded as full of tourists in the summer season.

From the cog railway depot in Manitou Springs to the summit of Pikes Peak is a 7,400-foot elevation gain. Pikes Peak rises dramatically above the city of Colorado Springs and is the highest summit of the southern Front Range of the Rockies.

Four of us agreed to go. In addition to Cory and me were Jim Vickery and John Clark. It was an easy hike up the six miles from Manitou Springs to Barr Camp, at 10,200 feet, where we had been given permission to spend the night in the Barr Camp cabin.

That night after a dinner of Dinty Moore beef stew cooked on our Primus stoves in the rustic cabin's kitchen, we were reclining comfortably when Cory sat bolt upright and exclaimed, "Did you hear that? Something is in our kitchen!"

"Come on, Cory, you're hearing things," I replied.

After a few minutes we all heard it. Jim jumped up and ran into the kitchen.

"Huge rats! They've taken one of our mess kit plates and are trying to get something else!"

"Throw something at him!" Cory shouted as he jumped up to go see.

Jim threw another mess kit plate at the pack rat, which ran quickly away and scurried up into the rafters.

"Let's keep all of our stuff over here by our sleeping bags," suggested John. We did. But all night long we could hear the rats in the ceiling structures above us. Sometimes we heard them come down into the kitchen again looking for loot.

The next morning after our breakfast of Grape-Nuts and canned Carnation milk, Cory advised, "I think we should put all our stuff into our backpacks and leave them outside somewhere. I don't want any pack rats rummaging through my stuff while we go for the summit."

We all agreed. We did not expect any other hikers to be coming by that cold winter day. Anywhere outside would be okay and better than inside the cabin.

We set out for the summit. One backtracks a short distance south and then follows the well-worn trail up to the top of Pikes Peak. It was not a bad day, although cold, and we reached the top via the trail without encountering any blizzards. There were a few snowdrifts on the trail to negotiate but the AdAmAn climbers had broken through them just the week before.

We looked quickly at the closed summit restaurant building, which served summer tourists who drove up the road.

"I don't know about you guys," Cory said, "But I'm for getting down quickly and grabbing our backpacks and going on down all the way today. I don't want those pack rats running around above me for another night!"

No one disagreed. We headed down and out of there in a hurry.

* * *

In the spring of 1952, I was selected to go to Boys State, which would be held for a week in early June at Camp George West, east of Golden. It was run by a combination of the American Legion and the state of Colorado, and the students were selected from schools throughout the state. The students were assigned to barracks and submitted a slate of candidates for election to the real statewide offices. The winners then occupied those offices for a full day later in the week.

During a previous year at Boys State, Boulder High students Ross Tyler and Dave Forsythe had been elected as governor and lieutenant governor, and that had been big news in

Boulder. Ross Tyler was an athletic star at Boulder High, and Forsythe was tall and good looking.

Since I had grown much bigger, had a decent appearance, and had even gained some self-confidence, I decided to try to get elected to something. I quickly focused on the office of chief justice of the Supreme Court of Colorado. That may not be governor, I thought, but it was a high office. I reasoned that not too many others would try for it.

How to get elected? There were only two days of electioneering before everyone there would vote for the candidates for all the state offices. It occurred to me to promise my barracks' vote to those of four other barracks for their candidates for the office of governor if they would vote for me for chief justice of the Supreme Court. With the short election time span of just a few days, it might work. I then told my barracks to vote for the governor candidate from any one of the four other barracks.

I emerged as the Colorado Boys State chief justice of the Supreme Court. I greatly enjoyed going to the state capitol and spending a whole day presiding over the Supreme Court.

Although generally I do not like the limelight, I admit to liking the notoriety of being featured in Boulder newspaper articles for a few weeks afterward.

When I was over at the Vickerys' place a few days later, John approached me.

"I'm going to get some of you guys into the ATO Fraternity at CU with me," he said. "This Boys State election will help you get in, Gus!"

"Well John, thanks. My brother liked ATO."

18

T he school year of 1951–1952 concluded in June. The Summit Club found itself effectively put on hold for the sake of its young members learning to make a living. Jim and John, being now eighteen, were hired as hod carriers for their dad's stone masonry business. Their pay was the envy of us all.

"I would like to become a stone mason like you!" I told Howard one day.

"Thanks, Gus," he said. "But you should stay in school. You are good at it."

Skip Greene managed to get a job up at the Mountain Research Station of INSTAAR (Institute of Arctic and Alpine Research), near Nederland. He worked there as a maintenance man. He greatly enjoyed driving an Army Weasel up onto Niwot Ridge to service the recording stations up there.

"I can look right up at Navajo Peak, Gus! Want to come up with me one day?"

"You bet. Just tell me when!"

Cliff Chittim got hired at Gruen's Service Station at the corner of 13th and Pleasant Streets. "I need to start to save some money to go to CU," he confided.

"Will you try to major in engineering?" I asked. "I hear the CU Engineering School likes to flunk out half their freshman class."

"We can both make it, Gus. We're both good in math," Cliff replied.

My mother had heard about a job on the trail crew up at Rocky Mountain National Park. She offered to drive me up to Estes Park to talk to the superintendent about it before the end of the school year.

"Absolutely!" I responded without hesitation. "I can probably outwalk anyone right now."

It was an easy sell given my mountaineering skills, and I was offered a position on the spot. For me, it was a dream job. Once the school year ended, my mother dropped me off in Estes Park, where I would spend the summer. We trail crew members were housed in the park's barracks in Beaver Meadows, just west of Estes Park. We could get all our meals there, seven days a week, which meant that my wages could mostly be saved.

In the evenings after work, we walked a half mile down to the Rock Inn and danced with the girls who also worked jobs in Estes for the summer. The beer was 3.2 percent alcohol and plentiful.

There were two trail crew units. The two foremen, Ralph and Mel, were permanent park employees who worked as heavy equipment drivers for the national park the rest of the year. I was placed on Ralph's crew. Mel was of slight build and not an avowed hiker. Ralph was heavier and clearly not a hiker.

The first job for the trail crews every summer, in June, was to dig through the big snowdrifts that still covered some of the higher trails. In 1952 that assignment was given to Ralph's crew.

"Gus, we're going to drive up to Bear Lake and walk over the trail to Odessa and Fern Lakes and dig through those big snowdrifts that always come in. Can you take the crew down there from Bear Lake?" Ralph instructed. "I'll meet you at the bottom at the other side at the Fern Lake trailhead at the end of the day."

"No problem. What if we're not finished?"

"Just come on down to the trailhead anyway at quitting time. It will probably take you a week to clear the trail completely. You'll be going back up there until it's finished."

This was an understatement for sure. The drifts covered the trail as high as ten feet deep. The trail going down Fern Canyon was on a north slope, and it had not melted off at all.

It took us more than a week of shoveling, but it was great fun. Each day we did the full walk from Bear Lake over a small divide to the north and down Fern Canyon. The hiking consumed several hours itself, even if you moved rapidly. We just left our shovels and other tools beside the snowdrifts at quitting time.

"I hope the tourists like these deep snow trenches, guys!" I declared to the other crew members.

"They love them!" replied a crew member who had worked the job the year before. "That's what they come out here for!"

He was right. Every day several groups showed up, hiking over from Bear Lake, and we had to help them get down over our incomplete diggings.

After we finished that task, Ralph took me aside by the barracks.

"Gus, next I want you guys to dig out the trench in the snow going into Chasm Lake. Can you handle that?"

I knew that snowbank, a dangerous one above tree-line

with a big drop to your death or serious injury if you lost your footing. It was high up, around 12,000 feet, and just below Chasm Lake and the East Face of Longs Peak. My climbing buddies and I had crossed it many times on our climbs up the East Face of Longs.

"Sure. But I'm taking my ice ax and a rope along just in case, Ralph!"

"No problem, Gus. You'll need to keep the crew safe up there."

When our crew went up on the first day, everyone turned to me for the next move.

"Someone can go out there first with a belay from me," I declared. "After we get a small trench dug, we'll move further out and someone else can get in behind us and deepen the trench down to the ground. That way we can safely dig our way across. Just don't go out onto that snowbank unroped or you will fall a long way!"

It took us several days to trench and then widen the trail for hikers to have a safe trip up to Chasm Lake. Our excavated trail there was not as deep as the one we had done by Odessa Lake but it was more important for the advanced hikers and climbers. My mountaineering skills served our trail crew well that summer.

* * *

Also housed in the Beaver Meadows barracks that summer was the blister rust crew. These were tough guys, mostly young, who every day had to go out to some steep, rocky, bushy slope in the park and hunt out and pull all the *Ribes* plants. These nonnative plants were a secondary host for the blister rust fungus, which attacks and kills white pine trees.

"*Ribes!* Damn *Ribes* plants all day!" I still remember one of the blister rust crew saying in his sleep several nights during the summer.

The foreman of that crew was Jim Glendenning, a local Estes Park youth a few years older than I. We on the trail crew were happy to be not on the blister rust crew pulling *Ribes* plants all day. Jim was a climber and was intrigued when I told him about our climbing club in Boulder.

"How did you guys get together to form that club?" he asked me one day.

"It started way back in junior high, Jim. Synergy. Then one of the moms suggested we tab ourselves as a club."

"Very lucky for you guys, Gus. I was the only one in Estes Park High School who wanted to go climbing."

* * *

One night I was awakened in the barracks by a ranger I did not know.

"Gus, we need the trail crew's help on a rescue. Someone has fallen way up by Lion Lakes in Wild Basin," he said. "We need you guys to carry him out. Can you rouse some of your crew and get going now? Can you pile them into your van and drive them over to the trailhead? You will only need four of them, although six would be better to spell some of you coming out."

"Sure. It's a long way up to Lion Lakes. That's above Thunder Lake."

"Well, you can catch some sleep at the Thunder Lake cabin for an hour or two. I don't know any other way to do it," he said.

"Are you coming? We might need some medical help," I asked.

"Yes. I will drive over to the trailhead and hike in with

you."

I talked six crew members into getting up and going. The ranger had assured me that we would get overtime pay for our efforts. When we met the ranger at the Thunder Lake trailhead in the depths of the night, he gave us all headlamps. He then hauled out from his truck a stretcher that had been converted from a bicycle, with a flat canvas surface mounted onto two wheels.

"This is all we have to carry this guy out if he can't walk. From what reports I have, he has a broken leg," the ranger told us.

"Don't worry, sir! We have already worked the trail up to Thunder Lake this summer."

"Very good! How about on up to Lion Lakes?" he inquired.

"No idea. I have heard it's not much of a trail," I responded.

One of my crew members grabbed the bicycle-stretcher and slung it over his shoulders.

"Good going!" I praised his initiative. "We can trade off carrying that thing."

The ranger was in good shape and took the lead up the excellent trail. With all our headlamps on we could see fairly well. We soon passed Calypso Cascades, and the sound of those small rapids of upper North St. Vrain Creek were reassuring. The ranger angled to his right for the trail heading up to Thunder Lake rather than the one to Ouzel Lake.

After six miles we arrived at the Thunder Lake ranger cabin.

"I didn't take the trail up to Lion Lakes, which cut off a bit down the trail," the ranger explained. "After a couple of hours of rest here we can cut over to it."

We all napped on the ranger cabin floor or on the flat

ground outside for an hour. Then the ranger awakened us.

"It's not light out yet, but we better get up to this guy. His partner left him there all night to come out to the trailhead and call us."

The so-called trail up to Lion Lakes was only a mile, but the going was rough. The accident victim was very happy to hear us coming and called out to us.

"I'm over here! Great to see you guys!"

His leg was in a bad way. It was a compound fracture. The ranger expertly splinted his leg, and we then carefully loaded him onto our stretcher. Four of us grabbed the handles and started to make our way down. It was not possible to use the tires, so we just carried him.

"The footing is terrible!" one of my crew members and now a stretcher bearer complained.

"You better believe it!" I replied. "But we will have a good trail after a mile."

Soon we were back on the main trail.

"Anyone willing to spell two of us?" I asked the others.

With multiple exchanges of carriers, we found ourselves in three hours back at the Wild Basin trailhead.

"I'll tell the Park Service to give you guys the day off!" said the ranger. "And many thanks!"

* * *

A few weeks later I received a message at the park barracks to call Cory in Boulder. I found a phone. "Hi Cory. What's up?"

Cory had enrolled at Colorado State University for the coming school year but was still in Boulder. His climbing partner Lynn was still in Boulder too.

"We want to climb Stettner's Ledges on the East Face of

Longs this weekend. We're going to pick up Skip on Friday afternoon, and we can swing by the barracks to get you after work. Then we'll pack in to the ranger cabin at Chasm Lake and do the climb early Saturday. Do you want to join us?" Cory asked.

"You bet! I'll be ready!" I exclaimed. Since my trail crew job was Monday to Friday, my weekends were open for such adventure.

Stettner's Ledges were a series of little ledges and piton ladders that took you diagonally up from the snows below the East Face onto Broadway, which sits halfway up the East Face of Longs. It was a state-of-the-art technical climb.

On Friday evening, we arrived at the Longs Peak trailhead in Cory's Jeep station wagon, everyone in high spirits. We hit the trail, and as we approached Chasm Lake, Cory sang out, "Did your trail crew cut this snowbank for us, Gus?"

"You bet! Do you like it, Cory?"

"Sure! You did a good job. But you got paid, right?"

"Well, of course!

There was no rain, and it was quiet as could be as the great East Face of Longs Peak towered above us. We settled in for the night beside the ranger cabin, falling asleep beneath the twinkling stars. Waking to a clear dawn, we were eager to get moving and head vertical.

From Chasm Lake we headed up on snow to the base of the East Face. Once there, Cory and Lynn led up on the first rope. Skip and I followed on a second rope. Without incident but with a lot of groaning, we hauled ourselves up the piton direct-aid portions, and we were soon on the Broadway Ledge. From there it is an easier climb to the summit of Longs, at 14,256 feet.

Longs Peak is the highest point in Rocky Mountain National Park and the northernmost 14er in the Rockies. The first recorded ascent was in 1868 by American West explorer John Wesley Powell and his surveying party, who summited it from the south side. Even though we had all climbed Longs Peak before on various routes, it never felt ordinary. And the Stettner's Ledges route was a satisfying achievement for all of us. We felt jubilant.

"I'm for running down the cables!" Cory announced when we were ready to descend. The Cable route runs straight up the sloping North Face of Longs from the Boulder Field shelter and is the quickest descent from the summit.

"Let's go for it!" I responded.

In short order we were back down to the main trail off the Boulder Field. At its junction with the Chasm Lake Trail, we backtracked the short distance to retrieve our backpacks left beside the shelter. We had avoided the afternoon thunderstorms that frequently threaten Colorado climbers in summer. It had been a perfect day.

* * *

At summer's end, the Park Service offered me a job as foreman of a new, third trail crew for the following summer season, 1953. They had been impressed with my performance and knew I could outwalk anybody.

I accepted in advance, knowing that I would at least have room and board for the summer before I began engineering school at CU. My mother had already told me she planned to sell the trailer right after I graduated high school. She would move to Buffalo, Wyoming, where my brother's family was still living happily.

19

In the fall of 1952, following on the heels of my success at Boys State, I decided to again run for elected office—this time at my high school. I ran for and was elected vice president of the senior class of 1953. Art White, a nice fellow, was elected class president.

In my role as vice president, I didn't really have to do anything. Art was never indisposed. Still, it was nice to be recognized as a class leader.

Cliff meanwhile was elected head boy. That meant he represented the entire student body. With his gregarious nature, he loved it.

Now that I was a high school senior, I decided that I needed a car of my own, although on a small budget. Borrowing my mother's car and riding my bike were not always practical or desirable, and my hunger for independence was increasing. For $25 I managed to buy my first car, a 1933 Plymouth convertible coupe. Freedom! It was not a fancy car, but it served its purpose and I was satisfied.

Around this time, the Harvard Club of Denver contacted Boulder High's administrators and asked them to send three

outstanding seniors to Denver to be interviewed. I was selected along with Dave Swerdfeger and Frank Miller, and we
were to be driven down to Denver. It was implied that we
would be offered scholarships if we should apply to Harvard.

Dave and Frank and I met at Boulder High at the appointed time to wait for our chauffeur.

"Hi Gus," Dave said when I arrived. Frank gave me a big
smile. Both of them were star players on both the football and
basketball teams.

"You know, I don't feel right about this," Frank said. "I
don't want to go to Harvard!"

"We're doing this for Coach Lefferdink or whoever recom-
mended us," Dave offered. "I have no intention of going to
Harvard either!"

"Let's hear them out," I said. "But I don't want to go there
either!"

We enjoyed the recognition and the day with the Harvard
Club. All three of us were at our best. But on the way back to
Boulder, we quietly joked in the backseat about how we were
just "not the Harvard type." We did not want to be the talented but poor boys brought in to maintain the quality and
reputation of a rich kids' school. We spoke in soft tones so as
to not offend the chauffeur.

* * *

At Boulder High, there was a one-year music requirement
for all would-be graduates. Since I did not want to play in the
band or orchestra, I selected choir in my senior year. The senior choir director was Eva Musil. She was reputed to be quite
professional.

It turned out that I have an ear for music, previously un-
known to me. Perhaps my mother's piano playing had left a

positive mark upon me. Or I may have simply inherited her ear for music. I quickly adapted to the full choir practices. Some of those were designed to increase one's range of scale. I was able to do that.

As a result, Mrs. Musil invited me to bring my "fine baritone voice" as the fourth member of the barbershop quartet. Jim Huffman and Mark Mullin were the tenors, and Tom Baird and I would share the baritone and base voices. Tom took the most important of those two voices on each song. I did not mind and felt honored to be chosen. The other three guys all had some formal voice training, which I did not.

On Thursdays we choir students and Mrs. Musil all piled into a large bus and performed in Thursday assemblies at nearby high schools. Thursday assemblies were an established "big thing" at all the larger high schools in the region. All the students were given time off from classes to go to them.

Our barbershop quartet was called The Four Hoarsemen, and we were very well received everywhere. One of our opening songs was "Mosquitoes," which was a crowd favorite. Jim would start with a very high hum, then Mark a little lower down the scale, and then Tom and I hummed as high as we could comfortably maintain our tones from lower down on the scale.

It was so much fun and a delight for us Four Hoarsemen to perform to such appreciative crowds. It rounded out the beginning of a fine senior year for me.

* * *

That fall I quaiified for the cross-country team. This was a new team, and nobody really knew how to coach it. Mr. Swinscoe had just selected some of us from the track team who were not playing football. We did not have time to do a single practice run.

Still, we took third in the state meet held on the nearby golf course. I was not the best, but I finished in not-too-bad a position, which was good for the team summary. A junior named Tommy Thompson finished highest on our team. It turned out he had been jogging on his own all fall.

* * *

In our senior year at Boulder High, I helped save Skip's life. The preceding summer he had become enamored with an outdoorsy girl who was working a summer job at the Meeker Park Lodge Mountain Resort. They had spent all their days off together, hiking and exploring in the high country. But when the summer was over, apparently so was the romance. The girl headed off to college in the East, seeking new horizons.

Skip took the loss hard. Disconsolate and feeling defeated, he decided he would attempt the first winter ascent of the East Face of Longs Peak. He confided his plan to me, which was to climb up the North Chimney below the Broadway Ledge and then head up Kiener's route to the top of Longs. He said he would pack in to Chasm Lake on Friday evening and leave a tent there. If he succeeded, he would spend Saturday night back in the tent and hike out Sunday.

Before he left, Skip gave me a copy of a letter he was also going to leave in his bedroom at home. Written in his neat, left-slanted cursive, he stated that if he failed in the North Chimney route, he would defer farther south to Lamb's Slide and go up the snow to Broadway, attempting to reach the top by that route.

He closed the letter with the almost poetic and certainly dramatic statement: *"If I am not back by Sunday afternoon, then things are not what they should be."*

Saturday morning, I became quite concerned with what seemed to me Skip's near-suicidal state of mind. As the day progressed, I was worried enough that I decided to go up to look for him. It was late afternoon as I post-holed up the telephone line to Chasm Lake and found nothing. Any tracks, if they had been there, would have been blown away by the fierce wind blowing all weekend.

Then I backtracked back down to Jim's Grove and found Skip's tent. It was neatly pitched behind a shelter of stunted alpine trees. I looked in and saw no signs of Skip having returned from his attempt.

I turned around and retraced my steps up toward Chasm Lake and then went off to the right and higher to the Boulder Field shelter at 12,000 feet. I found nothing to indicate he had descended that way, according to his plan.

The cold biting wind and late hour finally forced me to turn around and rush down the phone line shortcut to the trailhead and drive back to Boulder. When I got back that evening, I called Rocky Mountain Rescue, and they assured me that they would go up the next morning to look for him and, if necessary, bring him down.

It turned out Skip had taken a fall in the North Chimney but was not badly injured. Then, according to his plan, he went up Lamb's Slide, a snow couloir above Mill's Glacier that takes you to the southernmost point of the Broadway Ledge. He was somehow able to get around the snowbanks that block the Broadway Ledge there, and after traversing Broadway he went up Kiener's route to the top.

The fall and wind and cold had gotten to him, but Skip still managed to come down the back side of Longs Peak on the

Homestretch slabs, which had been blown clear. He traversed the Narrows to enter the Trough, a roughly 1,000-foot drop down steep cliffs. By then he was exhausted and with frozen hands and feet. After passing through the Keyhole, he took shelter in the Agnes Vale Refuge at 13,000 feet.

Hoping to thaw his hands and feet, he lit his Primus stove. The conical top of the refuge had accumulated a lot of blown-in snow. Suddenly it all dropped on top him. Due to the raging storm outside, he chose to spend the rest of the night there in the piled-up snow.

Rocky Mountain Rescue found him the next day, delirious, wandering on the Boulder Field just below the Agnes Vale Refuge, and they brought him down to safety. Hospitalization and medical care managed to save all his toes and fingers.

The aftermath was something I did not expect at all. I don't know the exact details, but the girl soon reached out to Skip and they resumed their romance. Possibly she had learned of Skip's narrow escape from death or maybe she merely regretted their breakup. But she returned to Colorado the next summer and eventually she and Skip married.

* * *

In April of 1953, I received a call from Merle Lefferdink, dean of boys and chairman of the scholarship board, telling me to come down to the Elks Lodge the next evening to receive the Most Valuable Student Award. Each year, one student from the Boulder High senior class was chosen for this award. I would be given a $75 prize in addition to presentation of the award before the Elks attendees. Dean Lefferdink suggested I bring my mother along.

When I was standing there in front of the whole lodge,

Dean Lefferdink asked if I wanted to say anything as he handed me the check.

"Sure. My mother is here, and I thank her for all her help. And I thank the Elks for this honor."

That was it. My mother was very pleased. However, I did not tell anyone else about it.

A week later Tim Greider, the editor of the student newspaper, *The Owl*, met me in front of the school before classes began. Somewhat sheepishly, he began, "Gus, I think you are going to like this issue of *The Owl*. You are on the front page."

With that, Tim handed me a copy of the paper. *The Owl* had front-lined its April 17, 1953, issue with: "Gustafson, Koener Are Most Valuable Students."

"You didn't tell any of us!" Tim exclaimed.

"Right! I didn't know what it meant. And who made the selection?"

"The Elks Lodge Scholarship Board. I phoned them to ask how they decided, and they printed the answer here. Keep reading," Tim replied. I read, "on the basis of citizenship, leadership, personality, resourcefulness, patriotism, and general worthiness."

Tim grinned at me. I grinned back. "Well, that covers just about everything!" I laughed. Then I added, "Tim, you know that I got the Boulder High Boy or Girl of the Month Award for the month of January, 1953."

"That might have helped. It turns out Doris is valedictorian for our class, and you have the third-highest GPA," Tim clarified.

"Wow. I had no idea. But I did get mostly A's and B's," I replied.

"Good enough to be third highest in a graduating class of two hundred," Tim affirmed. "Doris will get the Boettcher

Scholarship, which will pay all her college expenses. You'll get the Joint Honor Scholarship, which will pay everything except room and board at any Colorado state university."

I could tell that Tim was genuinely happy for me. I thanked him sincerely.

I also realized for the first time that this scholarship would allow me to attend college at CU. In their divorce agreement, my mother had forced my father to leave a small trust fund at a local bank for my college expenses. But it turned out to be barely enough to pay my ATO Fraternity dues. It was the scholarship that would make college achievable for me.

* * *

Come spring, Coach Swinscoe had selected me to run on the mile relay team. I was a solid 440 man, but there was a star athlete, still a junior at BHS, who always won that race. He anchored the mile relay team to a good result. His name was Jim Burke, and he also was a state champion wrestler and a halfback on the football team. Of course he won the individual 440 race at every track meet.

We ran the mile relay in one meet in 3.44 minutes, a school record that year.

"Hey, Cory, our BHS team won the conference mile relay," I told Cory when I ran into him one day later that spring. He was already a freshman at Colorado State University up in Fort Collins.

"Way to go, Gus! My 880-yard relay team set the school record of 1:34.8 minutes last year. George Hall was on that team too!" Cory retorted, pleasantly and in good humor.

* * *

In the Boulder High School library, I had read every book I could find about Tibet and Central Asia. It became an obsession for me. I desperately wanted to go to Central Asia and climb mountains.

One author whose books I found intriguing was Sven Hedin. Hedin was a Swedish explorer who had made a lifetime work of daring and risky expeditions into Central Asia. His reputation was a bit sullied by his pro-German sentiments. He did not let that bother him and justified his position as good for the protection of Sweden from Russia.

From his books I learned about "The Great Game." Who would fill the political power vacuum of the vast high country of Central Asia? Turkey had played the role in ancient times. Then came the Mongols. Later Russia, Great Britain, and China had all vied to do so.

That had led to the British expeditions into Tibet at the turn of the century. The well-trained British invasion of Tibet under Younghusband in 1903–1904 defeated the primitive Tibetan Army at Gyantse and proceeded to Lhasa. The British incursion denied the Russians any political influence in that part of the great plateau of Central Asia. It also gave the British the discovery of the highest mountain in the world, which bears the English name of Everest.

I read about all the attempts to climb Mount Everest. I knew by name all the climbers who had tried and failed to reach the summit on their expeditions of the 1920s and 1930s. I knew all the route variations they had taken. Nepal had been politically closed, so all attempts had been made on Everest's North Face in Tibet.

Then Nepal opened the routes to Everest's summit from the south. The Swiss quickly formed an expedition in 1952, with all the climbers from Geneva, and reached the South Col at 25,938 feet. From a camp there they pushed higher until they had to turn back at 28,199 feet, less than 1,000 feet below Everest's summit.

Of course, in our evening sessions at the Vickery house, we had discussed the possibility of climbing Everest. We all wanted to.

"None of us knows how well we would do at altitude," I reminded everyone.

"We haven't had any problems yet!" retorted Jim.

"Yeah, but we've never gone much above 14,000 feet," said Cliff.

We young guys were at first heartbroken when the news came out on May 29, 1953, that Everest had been finally summited.

"Well, there goes Everest," John affirmed to the rest of us when news came that Edmund Hillary and Tensing Norgay had summited Everest from the new route up the South Ridge from Nepal.

"Too bad for the British!" Cory observed. "Hillary is from New Zealand and Norgay is from Nepal."

20

"You'll use your Joint Honor Scholarship to go to CU, right, Gus?" Cliff asked one afternoon that spring as we headed out the front doors of Boulder High into the bright sun.

"Right! You are going to CU too?"

"Yeah. It's sort of expensive with the tuition and all. But I plan to stay at home while I try to make it through," Cliff replied.

"Well, I'll try to save some money from working on the trail crew up at Rocky Mountain National Park again this summer. They gave me a foreman's job and a crew, so I will make a little more than last summer," I replied. "And I get free room and board up there."

Both Cliff and I had been accepted into the engineering school at CU. Jim and Bill Fairchild were also going to try CU. Skip would continue his position at INSTAAR. John Clark had managed to become the first climbing ranger at the Longs Peak Ranger Station. John Vickery was doing well in the College of Arts and Sciences at CU and would be a junior there. George Hall had gone to Dartmouth. Lynn was talking about joining the Air Force.

"Will you join ROTC?" Cliff asked, as we lingered beneath the shade of some trees bordering the school lawn. "I will, for sure."

"No, I'm going to wait and see," I replied.

"John is in the Air Force ROTC, and Bill plans to join one of the service ROTCs. Jim is excused from any military service due to his broken neck from football," Cliff reminded me.

"Korea is winding down. Eisenhower seems to have gotten a cease-fire there," I observed.

As I turned to grab my bike and head home, Cliff had another question. "How hard do you think engineering school will be, Gus?"

"Very hard! That's another reason to not mess with ROTC right away. We both better really go for it our freshman year, Cliff."

I felt imbued with the reinforcement that the Joint Honor Scholarship gave me. But I also had a sense of the competition that faced us. Cliff read my mind.

"We face some bright guys from all the high schools in the state of Colorado," Cliff said. "The bright guys will mostly go to engineering school."

"Some of the bright guys will go down to the School of Mines," I countered. "I thought about going there. They carry twenty-two-hour course loads."

"I'm glad you're sticking with CU. But why didn't you go to Mines?" Cliff asked. "They have a great reputation."

"Good question, Cliff. Frankly, I think I know how to survive financially better here in Boulder. Also, I know the local terrain!"

* * *

"Let's celebrate graduation by sleeping on top of the Third Flatiron," Jim suggested as we hung out one evening in the Vickerys' small basement bedroom.

"Great idea!" John agreed. "We'll invite everyone. I haven't seen some of you guys for a while."

Eventually, eight of us agreed to the plan, and on Saturday afternoon we congregated at the Vickerys' house on Eighth Street. Piling into two 1940 Fords (Jim's and Skip's), we drove up to the Bluebell Shelter in high spirits.

"Where exactly will we sleep up there?" Bill Fairchild asked as we assembled for the climb. Bill was the least experienced climber among us and, not surprisingly, the least confident.

"We'll find you a good ledge and tie you in with pitons!" Jim replied. "Just be careful climbing up."

"There's a cave up there where the first and second pinnacles join near the top. Some of us can sleep in there," John Clark suggested.

"Should we bring ropes?" Cliff asked.

"Yes, bring some climbing gear. We may have to tie ourselves in for the night," Jim said.

The day was warm, and it did not look like rain would come that night.

"Smart of you guys to wait until later in the afternoon to avoid other climbers on the rock," Cory said.

"Well, we did not graduate from high school to be dummies!" Jim replied, laughing.

None of us bothered to rope up as we climbed up the face of the Third Flatiron, a climb most of us had made many times. As Jim topped the second pinnacle, he shouted down to encourage Bill, who was carefully following Cliff up the holds.

"Take your time, Bill! I've got a nice ledge for you up

here!"

Soon we were all there, crowded on top of the second pinnacle.

"We came up through the cave. I think I spied a good sleeping place there," John Clark declared.

"I might join you there after a bit," said Cliff.

"How about me?" Bill inquired.

"I think you should stick with the guys on top," Cliff replied. "They can tie you in."

The rest of us searched around for a small ledge somewhere atop the second pinnacle.

"Tomorrow morning I may climb up the First Pinnacle and rappel down from the top of it to wake you guys up!" Cory joked, as we set up our limited gear.

"Why don't you go sleep up there tonight," John Clark shot back. "You can be all alone!"

"No thanks! I don't want to miss out on any of the food tonight!"

Jim had managed to balance his small Primus stove on a little flat place. It hummed along as he offered warm sizzling slabs of Spam to everyone.

Night fell and the eight of us were alone together on top. There was no one else on any of the Flatiron pinnacles or on any of the nearby rocks. Green Mountain swallowed us into its darkness.

Below a mile in front of us, the lights of Boulder were shining.

"Should we sing something?" Cliff suggested.

"No. Let's keep it quiet," John Vickery said.

The occasional wind gust kept us aware of our delicate balances atop this dramatic pinnacle, which was assuming more and more mystery as dark enveloped us. No moon was to appear that night. Glittering stars above gave us all a sort of twilight to help us manage our balance.

"Sure wouldn't want to have to climb down tonight!" Bill observed.

"Wouldn't be any problem. Just use your flashlight," said Skip.

"Have any of you guys realized how lucky we are that nobody among us has died climbing?" Bill continued.

The rest of us were silent. We had climbed for the joy of it. We had never burdened ourselves by thoughts about luck or death.

"I almost got it when I went out of control glissading off Humboldt!" Cory finally offered.

"How could you die on a molehill like Humboldt?" exclaimed John Clark, who could not contain himself.

"We thought we could glissade anything! We all would see a steep couloir and just jump into it!" I added.

"That's right!" John Clark agreed. "Remember Mount Elbert? You just head north on its summit ridge and jump on several snow slopes to descend most of the way to the valley."

"Okay, okay. But those snow slopes were soft. On Humboldt, I happened onto glare ice." Cory looked at all of us, begging forgiveness.

* * *

It was not cold and no one had crawled into his Army surplus mummy bag yet. Besides, who wanted to start a long night trying to sleep while tethered by a piton and sling to some nearby crack in the summit rocks?

"Tell us a story, Jim," said Cliff.

"Yes, Jim, tell us one," John Clark seconded.

Jim's solemn face could be seen over the small flashlight he had installed in a crevasse near his perch.

"Are you guys all tethered?" he asked. We assented. We all had pounded pitons into small cracks and tied ourselves to them with one eighth-inch alpine cord.

"If I jumped off, I don't think this little alpine cord would hold me!" Skip joked.

"Well, then, don't jump!" John Vickery admonished.

"No one is going to push you," said Cory.

Silence surrounded us. There was a small breeze, but it wasn't going to blow anyone off their ledges.

"Okay, here's a story," Jim began. "It's about some guys who got together to do some climbing."

We all waited.

"They decided one spring vacation to go over to Aspen and climb the 14er Castle Peak on skis."

"I remember that!" Cliff exclaimed. "That 14er that's up above Ashcroft!"

Jim continued. "Do you remember Stuart Mace's place in Ashcroft?"

"Yes!" Cliff answered. "I remember you among the malamute sled dogs. One had his paws on your shoulders and was looking down at you!"

"Well, this gang of guys wanted Stuart Mace's okay to go up Castle Creek and put in a camp. They asked him, and he made a deal. It would be okay if they would break trail for his dogs through the foot of new snow that had fallen the night before. He would put our backpacks on his sled and go up with us."

"That was hard work! There was more than a foot of new snow," Skip recalled.

"But what fun! We found a great campsite just below Star Peak. Still in the trees," Jim continued. "And the weather was blue sky. Perfectly clear and the sun was shining."

"I remember you walking on your hands in that clearing

where we were setting up camp," Cliff added. "I also remember Stuart Mace helping us while his dogs rested."

"Yes. Mace thought he owned the whole Castle Creek Valley, the way he looked after it," I put in. "He had moved his sled dogs there from Boulder when the Aspen powers-that-be invited him to bring his dog teams over."

The breezes picked up for a few minutes as we all were lost in a reverie about our trip up Castle Peak. Breezes are a part of mountaineering in Colorado. You don't feel at home without them.

"Next morning we were up early and strapped on those long white Army surplus skis and headed up the valley from camp," Jim continued.

"Right! And cable bindings! I had big trouble getting used to those huge skis," I added.

"Do you remember the Montezuma hut? Right at timberline?" Jim asked.

"It was an A-frame, wasn't it?" Skip asked.

"Yes. Mace would give his clients a ride or ski up that far and put them up there for the night," Cliff recalled.

"When we got there, I was a bit behind you guys," I admitted. "But I still remember that huge Montezuma Basin opening up above timberline. I could see all of you mushing on up."

"Usually you are in the lead," replied Cliff.

"Right. I remember you staying behind with me as I struggled with those darn monster skis," I continued. "I still remember you saying 'We're gaining on 'em, Gus!' Thanks for that"

"It was 13,500 feet at the saddle. I figured we could all continue to the summit even though it was snowing all around us," Cliff agreed.

"Yes, we were all climbing individually by then," Cory recalled. "We left our skis at the saddle."

"I still remember us all sitting together on the summit in the snowstorm," said John Vickery. "Once we were all there, we started down quickly!"

"And it was getting cold! Cold!" said Cliff.

"It was a free-for-all skiing down that huge basin from the saddle," Skip laughed.

"Well, we were not exactly skiing experts," John Vickery chided.

"But we all got down!" Cliff returned.

The breezes picked up to a slight roar for a minute and then subsided again.

Jim was silent. The reminiscence was over. Jim had taken us all down Memory Lane.

Then Jim continued, "You know, we had so many great times. We never wasted our time swilling beer and chasing girls like most of those guys in high school."

We felt the truth of Jim's words and all nodded or murmured in assent. Darkness overtook us as we sat on our precarious perches. The night continued as the eight of us continued to sit in quiet appreciation in our heaven, not wanting it to end.

Acknowledgments

I thank my dedicated editor and friend Jillian Lloyd for her skills and patience with me.

To my youthful climbing buddies, how lucky we all were to have each other. I commemorate each of you.

I gratefully acknowledge Fate, which protected all of us from death or serious injury during our climbs.

Then there are the mountains. Who would we all be if not shaped by those magnificent contours of the Earth?

About the Author

Karl Gustafson is a professor emeritus of the Mathematics Department of the University of Colorado, where he taught for more than fifty years, until his retirement in 2020.

He was born in 1935 in Manchester, Iowa, and moved with his family to Boulder in 1948. As a pioneering young rock climber, Gustafson and his companions were at the forefront of the sport of free climbing in the region.

Gustafson graduated from Boulder High School in 1953 and from the University of Colorado in 1958. He earned his PhD in mathematics from the University of Maryland in 1965, after serving in Naval Intelligence. Following postdoctoral work in Switzerland and Italy, in 1968 he returned to Boulder, where he continues to live. He became the honoree of an endowed faculty chair at the University of Colorado in 2022.

Gustafson's previous books include *Introduction to Partial Differential Equations* (Wiley 1980, Dover 1999), *The Crossing of Heaven: Memoirs of a Mathematician* (Springer 2012), *Antieigenvalue Analysis: With Applications to Numerical Analysis, Wavelets, Statistics, Quantum Mechanics, Finance, and Optimization* (World Scientific 2012), and *Reverberations of a Stroke* (Springer-Nature 2019).

.

www.ingramcontent.com/pod-product-compliance
Lightning Source LLC
Chambersburg PA
CBHW052011030426
42334CB00029BA/3177